Fred Archer

by John Welcome

*

Novels

RUN FOR COVER
STOP AT NOTHING
BEWARE OF MIDNIGHT
HARD TO HANDLE
WANTED FOR KILLING

General Books

CHEATING AT CARDS—THE CASES IN COURT
THE CHELTENHAM GOLD CUP, THE STORY OF A
GREAT STEEPLECHASE (Constable)

edited by John Welcome

BEST SMUGGLING STORIES
BEST RACING AND CHASING STORIES
(with Dick Francis)
BEST MOTORING STORIES
BEST SECRET SERVICE STORIES I, II AND III
BEST GAMBLING STORIES
BEST HUNTING STORIES
(with Vincent Orchard)
BEST CRIME STORIES
BEST CRIME STORIES II

Fred Archer in Lord Hasting's colours after winning the Derby on
Melton: 1885

Fred Archer
HIS LIFE AND TIMES

John Welcome

FABER AND FABER LTD
24 Russell Square London

First published in mcmlxvii
by Faber and Faber Limited
24 Russell Square London WC1
Reprinted mcmlxvii
Printed in Great Britain by
Latimer Trend & Co Ltd Plymouth

Author's Note

I wish to acknowledge with thanks the permission of Messrs. J. A. Allen & Co. Ltd. to quote from the Hon. George Lambton's *Men and Horses I Have Known*.

I also wish to thank all those who answered my letters and helped me with this book, Mr. Robert Fellowes, the Agent of the Jockey Club who gave such ready assistance regarding the illustrations and other matters concerning Newmarket, and Captain Denis Baggallay, The Keeper of the Match Book in Dublin, for giving me access to the relevant volumes of the Racing Calendar, Mr. J. A. Allen and Mr. R. E. Way for searching for out-of-print books, Dick Francis for reading the typescript and once again, too, I have to express my gratitude to the indefatigable Mrs. Joan Saunders of the Writer's and Speaker's Research without whose ready co-operation and prompt and accurate help this book could never have been completed.

J.W.

Illustrations

Fred Archer in Lord Hastings's colours after winning the Derby
on Melton: 1885   *frontispiece*

Chapter 1

He was nervous, shy, introspective and highly intelligent. These qualities were not inherited from his father, whom he resembled neither in looks nor in temperament. William Archer, the jockey's father, was one of thirteen children. He was born on 1st January 1826 at St. George's Cottage, St. George's Place, Cheltenham, where his father kept a livery stable. Small, almost squat, with tiny hands and feet, he was a rough man both in appearance and habits. Himself a jockey of the old school, short-tempered, hard-swearing and pugnacious, he boasted that he had not had more than two days' schooling in his life. His boast may well have been largely true for at the age of eleven he ran away from his parents and managed to secure employment riding for a Mr. Eccles of Birmingham. At first his career was successful and indeed colourful. Although jockeys in those days earned very little—one of William Archer's engagements being for a salary of £6. os. od. a year and a suit of livery—he rode enough winners to keep him going. Soon, however, trouble with his weight turned his thoughts towards steeplechasing. Again success followed him and he attained prominence, so much so that when the Emperor of Russia was looking for someone who would manage his stud and ride his horses William Archer was asked if he would consider taking the position. He accepted and at the age of seventeen, with testimonials from the Earl of Chesterfield and the Marquis of Anglesey he sailed from Hull with sixteen English thoroughbreds under his care. His quarters were at the Tsarskoe Zelo Palace near St. Petersburg and for two years he trained the Czar's horses there and at Thirsk, near Moscow. But the cold climate affected his health so he returned to Cheltenham and took up again the hard grind of life as a professional jockey over fences. A fine horseman with an unshakeable nerve and a way of getting on with owners and trainers, success came back to him quickly.

In 1849 he married Emma Hayward, the daughter of William Hayward, the sporting owner of the King's Arms, Prestbury, near Cheltenham. He was fortunate indeed in his choice of wife. Emma Hayward was an aristocratic-looking, soft-voiced, sweet-natured woman. The couple went to live at the family home at St. George's Cottage. Here their two daughters were born, followed by their first son, William. The second son was also born at St. George's Cottage on 11th January 1857. He was christened Frederick James Archer.

In the following year, 1858, William Archer fulfilled the culminating ambition of every steeplechase rider then as now when he won the Grand National on Little Charlie. He was thirty-two years of age, and after this success he moved to Prestbury where his third son Charles Edward Archer was born on 22nd December 1858.

By now the hardships of his career and the demands of his family were beginning to tell. Steeplechase jockeys have always earned less than their more fashionable brethren on the flat and in those days the rewards of even a famous jumping jockey were meagre indeed. Archer looked about for some other means of supplementing his income and securing his family. When the opportunity came of taking over his father-in-law's house, the King's Arms, it seemed that he had found it. He rode less and less and in 1862 gave up altogether, his last mount being in a race at the long-forgotten meeting at Beckford on a horse called Little Dwarf.

Fred Archer's early years were dominated by his father. Having had little or none himself William did not believe in the value of education for his sons. Fred went, on and off, to the village school, but books were not to be allowed to interfere with the real business of life which, in William's eyes, was that of riding a horse.

Fred had brains and later on he knew it, so that to the end of his days he was bitterly to regret this lack of education. His handwriting remained always childish and unformed. He was utterly unable to express himself on paper though he was fluent and explicit in conversation. Much later his solicitor put it on record that Archer had distinct difficulty in writing anything other than his name and that even his signature was made with some trouble. Save for a few boyhood scrawls his family had virtually nothing from him in his own handwriting and in later life, if letters had to be written, he frequently had a friend of his, Joseph Davis, to write them for him.

William Archer kept the King's Arms for seven years but, as might be expected, he was no business man. He was, as many of his kind are and were, feckless about money. When it was there it slipped through his fingers and when it was not he lived on what credit he could. Difficulties began to encompass him, debts mounted up and creditors became pressing. These matters confined his activities and reduced his circumstances but they had little effect on his spirits for William Archer was physically and mentally tough whereas his second son was neither. As Fred began to grow into boyhood it was seen that in appearance and disposition he took after his mother. He was tall where his father was short; his features long and distinguished where his father's were round and rough; he was soft-spoken and highly-strung where his father was loud-voiced and resilient.

His mother doted on him. She wanted him to be educated and to bring him up to better himself in the world. When she protested about his lack of formal schooling William's reply was brusque and to the point. 'Let the lad alone; he'll make more out of his riding than he ever will out of book-learning,' he said. He was to live to see his prophecy more than amply fulfilled.

For William could recognize ability as a rider and promise as a jockey when he saw it, and in young Fred he knew immediately that he had something quite out of the ordinary. His methods of tuition were, as might be expected, rough and ready, but they were also effective.

At first the lessons took place in the garden at the King's Arms. William would lunge the boy's pony, a Galloway called Chard which he had won in a raffle, over a small hurdle he had put up, shouting and cursing at him all the time until he was satisfied with his seat. They then moved to Prestbury Park racecourse where the coaching consisted of William throwing pieces of grass and turf at boy and pony indiscriminately and shouting instructions, adjurations and bad language at them both. It was said that Fred on these occasions was a great deal more frightened of his father than of either the pony or a fall.

Extraordinarily enough, his natural aptitude triumphed over his nervous temperament and his abilities thrived and burgeoned under this draconian régime. Soon he was accompanying his father to meets of the Cotswold Hounds. At one of these his riding career was nearly finished before it began. In a gateway during a check a horse kicked him and broke his leg badly. It mended, however, better and more quickly than anyone expected and at eight years of age his father put him up in his first race. It was a match, his pony against a donkey at a local sports meeting. The course was twice round an orchard of the Plough Inn with a brook to be jumped each time. He was carefully fitted out in colours and breeches but, despite this, the other rider, who was described as a yokel brandishing a thick stick, beat him by a neck. Archer came home crying, whether from disappointment, for he was never to the end of his days a good loser, or fear of his father, will never be known. Shortly afterwards he did, however, win a donkey race round a paddock at the Plough Inn and this is the great jockey's first recorded victory.

The following year, 1866, when he was nine years old, his father gave his friend Charles Pullen, another innkeeper who was landlord of the Unicorn at Winchcombe, five pounds for a blood pony for the boy. This pony stood 12·2, they called her Moss Rose and entered her in a pony race at Malvern, Fred Archer up. There is no record of what happened in that race so presumably they were unplaced. Moss Rose, although Archer hunted her and went brilliantly to hounds on her until he left home to be apprenticed, was never an easy ride. Once she took him over the rails in a race. He turned her round and jumped back on to the course and, so the story goes, finished second.

It was his performances out hunting which determined his future career for he caught the eye of the two La Terrière brothers, both of whom had ridden under Rules in their younger days as Gentlemen Riders. The two Archers, William and Fred, and the two Owens, Roddy and Hugh, together with the young La Terrière used, in the words of Colonel de Sales La Terrière writing many years afterwards, 'to shove along against each other' out hunting. There was certainly a wealth of riding talent in the young entry of the Cotswold Hunt of those years for, besides Fred, his brother was to become a well-known rider on the flat and over fences and the names of Hugh and Roddy Owen— certainly of Roddy—are among the immortals of steeple-chasing.

One day in November 1867 Mr. 'Dick' La Terrière fell in with Fred and his father coming home from hunting. The talk turned on Fred's future and William Archer said he wanted to make the boy a jockey. Mr. La Terrière made the suggestion that he would write to Mat Dawson, the Newmarket trainer, to see if he would take Fred on as an apprentice. This he did and either his recommendation carried considerable weight or else William Archer's name was still remembered with respect among racing people, for the reply came back almost immediately to send the boy along.

William didn't send him; he brought him. This was in February 1868 when the boy was eleven years old, exactly the same age as that at which his father had run away from his parents to seek fame and fortune on the racecourse. The first week of his son's new life William spent at Heath House, Mat Dawson's establishment, watching Fred ride out with the string and being introduced to his duties.

Although at this time Dawson had not been long at New-market his name stood high in his profession. Naturally enough he was bombarded with applications and entreaties to take on boys, many of which he almost automatically refused. Yet he took young Archer apparently on request and without refer-ences or further inquiry. All this, together with the length of William Archer's stay at Heath House, lends colour to the sup-position that there was at least some acquaintanceship between them. Formal indentures were entered into on the 10th February 1868 by which '*Frederick Archer now or late of Prestbury near Chel-tenham of the age of eleven years or thereabouts doth put himself apprentice to Mathew Dawson of Newmarket All Saints in the County of Cambridge training groom to learn his Art . . . to serve from the day of the date hereof until the full end and term of Five Years from thence next following to be fully completed and ended.*

'*During which term the said apprentice his Master faithfully shall serve his secrets keep his lawful commands everywhere gladly obey . . . he shall not commit fornication nor contract matrimony during the said term he shall not play at cards or dice tables or any other unlawful games whereby his Master shall have any loss . . . he shall not haunt taverns nor playhouses nor absent himself from his said Master's service day or night unlawfully. . . . He the said Mathew Dawson will pay unto the said Fred Archer the undermentioned wages that is to say seven guineas for the first year nine Guineas for the second year eleven guineas for the third year and thirteen guineas for the Fourth and Fifth year respectively and his said apprentice in the Art of a Jockey and Trainer of racehorses which he uses by the best means that he can and shall teach and instruct or cause to be taught or instructed finding unto the said Apprentice sufficient meat drink and also hat coat and waistcoat in each year and lodging during the said term. . . .*'

If, as it turned out, Dawson was fortunate in his apprentice, Archer was lucky indeed in that day and age to have found such a master.

Mathew Dawson, though not yet at the pinnacle of his fame

1. Archer's Indentures

2. Three Spy cartoons:
(*Right*) George Fordham
(*Below*) Fred Archer and
George Abingdon Baird

in the year Archer joined him, had already made his name renowned in his profession both for integrity and ability. He
came from Gullane in Scotland and had been born into a family
of horsemen and trainers. His father had been one of Scotland's
leading trainers and his three brothers all achieved success in the
same profession. 'Their manners are courteous, their stable
management has passed into a proverb, and their judgement of a
yearling is held in as high repute as their irreproachable taste for
whisky,' was how *Bailey's Magazine* most accurately summed
them up.

After commencing training in Scotland Mathew came south
as a young man. He set up at Russley Park near Lambourn as
private trainer for Mr. Merry, a Scottish ironmaster who had
bought the mares belonging to Lord John Scott, one of Dawson's
early patrons. Here his first really important successes were
gained and for Mr. Merry he won many races including the St.
Leger with Sunbeam in 1858 and the Derby with Thormanby
in 1860. But differences arose between them. Merry was never
an easy man to serve, and Dawson was finding Russley too remote and isolated. He terminated his engagement with Mr.
Merry and set up as a public trainer at Newmarket, taking over
the tenancy of Heath House when his brother Joseph left it.

Rich and aristocratic patrons followed him there including
the Dukes of Hamilton and Newcastle, and his success was
immediate. He was a hard, uncompromising man who cared
little for money but a great deal for winning races. His adminis-
tration of Heath House was lavish, his attention to detail meti-
culous. He retained to the end of his days the blunt out-spoken-
ness of the Lowland Scot and he was no respecter of persons however highborn even though those were the days when privilege
stalked openly in the corridors of power and when weaker
characters who chanced to offend were ruthlessly suppressed and
often ruined by the ruling establishment.

His Sunday afternoon nap was sacrosanct, and woe betide
anyone who dared to disturb it. Once a noble owner with a
large string of horses in the yard came to see them after lunch on

a Sunday. He sent for Dawson and insisted on his coming out to speak to him. At length Dawson did so. 'You want to see your horses today,' he growled. 'You can see them tomorrow to take them away.'

He despised weakness either in men or horses. Once the Duke of Portland, then probably his richest and most important owner, purchased a well-bred filly and asked him to admire her. Dawson ran his eyes over her and said bluntly: 'She's a damned bad specimen of a damned good breed, Your Grace.' Beneath his gruffness, as often happens, lay a kind heart, but it took some finding for he was a hard taskmaster. Much of his success, as in the case of all great trainers, lay in his ability to time his training of a horse right up to the very day of the race. But to ensure that this was done meant, according to the methods of the day, that the horses in his care were asked to stand up to a most severe preparation. So were the men.

Racing stables in those times were indeed hard nurses of men and it is not surprising that it took young Archer some time to recognize his good fortune. He was desperately lonely, home-sick and unhappy. Thin, gangling, over-grown and frightened, he was bullied unmercifully. He wrote to his mother short, scrawled, half-illiterate notes entreating her to take him away, to allow him to come home. Every morning he was in tears before he rode out. But despite his nerves and the bullying he went on doing his two and riding with the string, keeping his place, doing what he was told, and learning his job.

Gradually the constant torture from the other boys stopped, to be replaced by something like respect. For the fact was that nervous, highly-strung and delicate though he appeared to be he was prepared to get up on anything and, once up, to master it. It was soon seen that horses went for him that would not go for others and that, once in the saddle, his nervous apprehension disappeared to be replaced by determination and skill.

John Corlett, the owner and editor of *The Sporting Times*, affectionately called *The Pink 'Un* from the colour of the paper on which it was printed and which was so beloved by the

Bohemians in those far-off days, on one of his rounds of the racing stables paid a visit to Mat Dawson not long after Archer had started his apprenticeship.

As the two men were casting their eyes over the string Dawson pointed to Archer. 'I shall make a jockey of that lad some day,' he said to the editor. 'He is the pluckiest I ever had. He will do anything.' Dawson then did what to modern eyes must appear a most extraordinary thing. Archer was riding a bay horse called St. Pancras which was being trained for the flat. Calling him out of the string Dawson said to him: 'Ride him over that fence into the next field, Archer. Your father used to ride over fences and I don't see why you shouldn't.'

Archer promptly did so and then jumped back again and rejoined the string.

Corlett never forgot the incident, saying many years afterwards that his first knowledge of Archer was 'stamped in a most peculiar manner' on his memory. It is an apt enough comment, and the little scene well demonstrates the demands Dawson made on his men and his horses and the unquestioning way in which Archer was prepared to obey them.

Dawson, in fact, had an almost infallible instinct about both men and horses. He could sense the weakling or the rogue of either species within a minute or two and neither was allowed near his stable or, if by any mischance one did get in, then he was very speedily cast out—whatever rank or wealth he could command. From the first he seems to have divined the promise latent in the slim, nervous, almost ladylike youth who had been entrusted to his care. It was only a step from admiring that promise and the courage with which Archer overcame his fears to being attracted by his quiet demeanour and pleasant personality.

Dawson and his wife were childless. Soon an attachment all the more deep and steady because it was unspoken sprang up between the three of them. But Dawson was the last man to show favouritism. There were strict rules in the stable over and above the usual routine and discipline. No horse must be sworn at or badgered about by the lads; a stick must not be used without express permission. Had Archer broken either of these injunctions or absented himself from daily prayers, retribution would have been swift and ruthless. There was a stiff wire fence round the house and stables to keep the lads in at night and Dawson probably never knew to the day he died that Archer along with the others had found a way of climbing out and in as he liked.

He was, however, in everything else a model pupil. Even at that early age he was possessed by the lust to succeed. He wanted desperately to get on in the world, to make his name and to make a lot of money. Certainly he was progressing all the time in the esteem and affection of the Dawsons not, perhaps, entirely without calculation for, as Lambton says, he had an eye to the main chance.

It was, just the same, over a year after he joined the stable that he was allowed home to see his family again for a short holiday. It was during that same year, 1869, that something happened which was to have a decisive effect on his career and his fortunes. Lord Falmouth decided to send his horses to Mat Dawson at Heath House.

Evelyn, sixth viscount Falmouth, of Mereworth Castle and elsewhere, had been at the Bar when he unexpectedly and through the death of a cousin, came into the title. His marriage a little later to Mary Frances Elizabeth twenty-third Baroness Despencer in her own right brought him great estates and Mereworth Castle in Kent where he set up his stud. A quiet unassuming man of high intelligence and integrity he ran his horses at first under the *nom de course* of 'Mr. Valentine'. During that time they were trained by John Scott at Malton and it is said that the only bet which he ever had in his life was with his trainer's wife. This was for the sum of sixpence that his filly Queen Bertha, having already won the Oaks, would win the St. Leger of 1863. Queen Bertha was beaten by half a length by Lord St. Vincent's Lord Clifden and Falmouth presented Mrs. Scott with the sixpence made into a brooch set in diamonds. Queen Bertha later became the dam of Wheel of Fortune, a

[20]

mare which Archer was to bracket with St. Simon as one of the two best racehorses he ever rode. The association of Falmouth, Dawson and Archer, when it came about, was to prove one of the most brilliant and successful ever to appear on the English Turf.

That, of course, was all in the future when, in the spring of 1869, Archer returned from his holidays. He was twelve that year and he had his first mount in public. This was at the Newmarket second October meeting on a mare called Honoria in the Newmarket Town Plate. Fred Webb was at that time the stable's lightweight jockey. Honoria had been put in to make the pace for Lord Falmouth's Stromboli which Webb was riding. Another motive for entering her was that Dawson wanted to give his good apprentice a ride in public without putting too much responsibility on him. Archer did what he was told and made the running. The mare faded and finished last. Webb duly won for Lord Falmouth and everybody was pleased except possibly Archer who never took kindly to defeat in whatever guise it came.

His father, whose financial position was worsening with the years, became anxious to push the boy on. Shortly after the ride on Honoria he came to Newmarket on a visit to find out about his son's prospects and, in the course of this visit, they went to the sale of Mr. Naylor's horses. Here they fell in with a lady owner, a Mrs. Willan, who had ponies in training both on the flat and over fences and whose husband was a Steward under pony racing rules. Known as Mrs. 'Croppy' Willan because she cut her hair and wore gaiters she was a prominent racing figure and frequently came to Prestbury. Archer had some acquaintance with her and had run ponies of his against her in matches. He went straight up to her and said: 'If you are looking for someone to ride your steeplechasers, Madam, I have the very one to ride over fences for you.' And he pointed to his son.

As it happened Mrs. Willan was at just that moment searching for a lightweight to ride her well-known pony Maid of Trent in a steeplechase at Bangor. She went to Mat Dawson to ask for his recommendation and to secure his permission for Archer to ride. Both were most willingly given. Weighing out at the well-nigh incredible figure of 4 st. 11 lb. young Archer duly won the race for her. So the great jockey's first victory under any rules was at the age of twelve and in a steeplechase, and to Mrs. Willan belongs the honour of having put him up.

He had to wait some time—almost a year in fact—before riding his first winner on the flat. This was at Chesterfield on 28th September 1870. He did not ride his first winner for the Heath House stable though it was at the suggestion of Dawson that Archer was given the mount. The race was a nursery handicap for two-year-olds. Archer, carrying 6 st. 5 lb., won it on Mr. Bradley's Athol Daisy trained by John Peart at Malton, and the grateful owner, as a present for his win, sent a pound of green tea to his father! On the following day he rode her again in the Hartington Plate and finished second. He had not, however, long to wait for his next winner. On 14th October he won the Tay Handicap at the Caledonian Hunt Meeting on Lincoln Lass carrying 7 st. 10 lb., starting favourite and beating five other runners.

In this, the second year of his apprenticeship he had fifteen rides in public, two winners and was placed second nine times. It was not a bad average and, on the whole, a very promising start.

Chapter 2

But after that good start the year 1871 was a frustrating one. He had twenty-seven rides but only three of them were winners. Moreover, when on Lord Falmouth's Ortolan in the Great Eastern Railway Handicap at Newmarket First October Meeting he was reported along with another jockey called Wheeler by the starter for misconduct at the post. As a result the stewards of the meeting stood him down for a fortnight. This was the only occasion in his entire career that he suffered punishment or suspension from the Turf Authorities.

The frustration was all the more acute because demands for help were already beginning to come from home and he could do little or nothing about them. It was not until the following year that his big chance came. He grasped it eagerly.

A Mr. J. Radcliffe, otherwise known as 'Holy Joe', had a few horses in training with Mat Dawson. One of them was a colt called Salvanos. He fancied the colt for the Newmarket October Handicap at the first October Meeting of 1871 and he had a big bet. Salvanos, a very big, strong colt, was a difficult ride; he bolted with Chapman, the lightweight jockey who had been put up, and Holy Joe lost his money.

Admiral Rous, the great handicapper and dictator of the Turf, was at that time in his seventy-seventh year. Up till then the mistakes in his handicaps had been few and far between but it is probable that his hand and eye were beginning to lose their cunning. At all events he let Salvanos into the Cesarewitch at the minimum weight of five stone seven pounds, a piece of handicapping which did not escape criticism nor, needless to say, did it escape the eyes of Mat Dawson and Holy Joe Radcliffe. Mr. Radcliffe saw an immediate opportunity of retrieving his fortunes which were at that time going exceedingly badly, and Mat Dawson saw the winning of another big race handed to him, as it were, on a plate—if he could find a lightweight jockey capable of controlling Salvanos. It says much for his confidence in Archer and the way the boy's growing abilities had impressed him that he decided to advise Mr. Radcliffe to give him the mount. It says much, too, for Radcliffe's confidence in Dawson that he took the advice, for Archer was virtually unknown at the time and there was a very considerable amount of money at stake.

Although Salvanos made a determined effort to run out, he did not bolt with Archer. Even at that early age horses seldom did. That was the only real danger, for the horse was thrown into the handicap and all his connections knew it. Salvanos hit the front at the bushes, was never really challenged and won as he liked. 'Little Archer', a leading Turf authority wrote, 'rode Salvanos with the coolness and steadiness of a veteran, and thus early made his mark as one of the rising lightweights. He is altogether free from the "flashiness" of the modern school of "feathers" who have come to such utter grief before they are well out of their teens.'

Although it did draw upon him the attention of owners and trainers and the more knowledgeable of the racing public, it would be quite wrong to say that the winning of this race made Archer. Indeed there was an immediate rebuff in store. Salvanos, going up only seven pounds in the weights, was made a short-priced favourite for the Cambridgeshire. Starting at two to one against and ridden by Archer he ran unplaced and lost Mr. Radcliffe most of the money he had won on the Cesarewitch.

Still, twenty-five wins out of one hundred and thirty-six rides was not a bad average for the year and the number of his mounts in itself shows the increasing interest in his powers. The door to fame and fortune was just beginning to open, but more important still, at last there was something to send home to meet the demands of his parents.

In 1873 he was out of his indentures. Dawson presented him with a gold watch inscribed: *For good conduct—Mathew Dawson,* a present he was to treasure to the end of his life. Dawson also gave more tangible proof of his appreciation by appointing him as lightweight jockey to the stable in place of Webb who was having increasing difficulty with his weight.

Rides and requests for his services now came thick and fast. Already it was beginning to be realized that whether he won or not—and that year winners were at first slow in coming—he was always a trier.

Throughout his life he wanted above everything to win. He was driven on by ambition and he had to be in front. In his room at Heath House he would read and re-read the form; on the racecourse he watched and studied the running of every horse, working out a way to win on him were he asked to ride, or how to defeat him were he on another. Here his very considerable natural intelligence and acuteness helped. Owners and trainers even at that early age were struck by his articulate manner and the perceptiveness of his observation. When he dismounted he could tell them not only how his own horse had gone but pretty well how everything else in the race had run also, and what had happened during the running. This is unusual even now; then it was exceptional indeed.

He was helped, of course, by the slow pace at which races were run in those days, but even so the quickness of his appreciation and his ability to sum up any race over whatever distance whether he had ridden in it or not were quite extraordinary. To such a pitch did he bring this art that later on, during his years of fame, if he saw a horse which he thought should have won he would frequently go to the owner and ask to be allowed to ride it next time. Owners at that period of his career were only too pleased and flattered to have him ask to ride their horses— usually it was they who had to come searching for his services.

On these occasions he was almost always right and he would win the race. Indeed there was one plunger, George Wales, who followed him round, backing his mounts for enormous sums, sometimes up to as much as five thousand pounds and, during the years of Archer's greatness, amassing a fortune. This fortune, as is the way with most plungers, he failed to keep and he died in penury, as did Holy Joe Radcliffe, the owner of Salvanos, who ended up as a tipster.

It was during this period of his life, thinking out ways of winning races, that he adopted the policy of extreme punctuality. Invariably he was first into the parade ring, but more important still, he was first out of it, and first down at the post. In those days there was no draw for places. Thus he could take up the position he wanted at his leisure and in accordance with plans previously worked out for winning the race. Once he had taken up his chosen position he saw that he kept it and woe betide anyone who tried to take it from him. Already, too, he had perfected his quickness at getting away, though he took good care to see that the starter never had further opportunity to complain of his conduct.

Also, having learnt his lesson and with his eye firmly fixed on success and the main chance, he cultivated the acquaintanceship of Tom McGeorge the senior starter. The intimacy between them, which was almost certainly—on Archer's part at least—begun for business reasons, ripened into true friendship and the McGeorges, uncle and nephew, were to remain in the select inner circle of Archer's close friends until his death. McGeorge kept a hotel at Newark and Archer often stayed there with him if there was racing nearby. Both of them always maintained that their friendship made no difference to McGeorge's fairness at the start. Since McGeorge was universally respected for his firmness and lack of favouritism as well as his proven ability to get his fields away on level terms, no mean achievement in those days of starting flags and false starts, this is almost certainly the case but at least it can be said that the friendship did Archer no harm and in the days when he was looking for rides the fact that everyone knew of it was another encouragement for owners to seek him out.

All these things contributed to his increasing success. Once he had filled Webb's position the winners commenced to come in a steady flow. They were none of them in very important races as yet though he did win the Great Lancashire Handicap on Lord Falmouth's Kingcraft the Derby winner of 1870. In all he had four hundred and twenty-two rides and the season ended in a desperate race for the jockeys' championship between himself and Constable. He lost that race, Constable beating him by three, having one hundred and ten wins out of three hundred and ninety-seven mounts. It was the last time anyone other than Archer was to head the list for thirteen years.

Even though he was beaten it was a considerable achievement for a boy of sixteen only just out of his indentures, to go so close. But to do it he had been desperately hard on his horses. In those days jockeys rode in spurs—long, thin pieces of steel with sharp, wicked rowels. The whips, too, were long and fully deserved to be called cutting whips. They were slim and sharp and had no comfortable leather flap at the end, but tapered to a narrow point capable of biting right into the tender skin of a thorough-bred and raising blood with each well-directed stroke. Archer used both of these implements unmercifully.

The reputation for undue severity which he earned in his early years clung to him for the rest of his life and has followed him into history. But he was never a mere butcher. He had patience and was able, when he wished, to ride any sort of a race. He could wait or go on and he was always a superb judge of pace. Where he really excelled was in a finish, his long legs appearing to wrap themselves round the horse's sides and almost lift him to the post. Even there, in the actual method of finishing, he had thought the business out. His finishes were ridden on a loose rein and thus he was 'up the horse's neck' at the post. This, he maintained, was the right place to be for it caught the judge's eye, whereas Fordham, his greatest rival for most of his career, sat back at the finish and sometimes missed the verdict.

If he was hard on his horses he was doubly so on himself. His keen analytical mind went over every race he rode seeking the causes of victory or the reasons for defeat. His losing rides came in for more of his attention than his victories as he sought to find out why they had happened and where lay the blame. As with many introspective men he was too ready to accept the responsibility himself and to believe that defeat came from his own mistakes. This was another reason for his intense dislike of being beaten. Defeat brought on black moods of doubt and self-criticism which could only be dissipated by further victories. Thus he lived in a sort of vicious spiral where losses spurred him on to further and greater endeavours and these in their turn, by the wasting and intense nervous and physical effort they demanded of him, sometimes brought about defeat. All this had a part to play in the final tragedy.

In the season of 1873, besides his second in the jockeys' championship which seemed a certain pointer to future success, something else happened which was to have a decisive effect on his career. Tom French, the stable jockey to Heath House, died at the height of his powers. French was not unlike Archer in appearance, manner and style of riding. He was exceptionally tall for a jockey, very quiet and reserved on his feet, very determined and severe on a racehorse. It is almost certainly true to say that Archer modelled himself on French, as younger men often will adopt the style and methods of an older and successful member of their profession with whom they are brought into contact and whom they respect and admire. Indeed some of Archer's early severity may have come from copying his senior for French, when the occasion demanded, was merciless on his mounts. When he beat Fordham in a hectic finish for the Chevely Stakes in 1872 Sir George Chetwynd, looking at the winner's sides where French's whip had played havoc, commented that it could not be called a bloodless victory.

French, like Archer later, had to pursue a drastic course of wasting to ride at all. This brought on consumption. Despite the disease and knowing that he had it, he refused to give up his career. The deprivations to which he subjected himself only hastened the inevitable. He died that year at the age of twenty-nine, the very same age at which Archer was to perish from his own hand and from much the same basic causes.

At the commencement of the 1874 season the position of first jockey to Heath House was as yet unfilled. Archer's success of the year before had marked him as a coming man and such well-known racing personalities as Price Batthyany and the Earl of Rosebery had already given him minor retainers. Nevertheless he was still only seventeen and his average riding weight was a bare 6 st. In fact he could still do the minimum weight of 5 st. 7 lb. But he looked, and indeed was, an overgrown boy. If he were to be offered the position of stable jockey it was obvious that he was going to have to put up a considerable amount of deadweight in classic races and more still in some handicaps. This, together with his youth and inexperience, made Dawson hesitate about appointing him. But very quickly he made his claims clear.

There was then on the Turf a gambling owner called Frederick Swindell. Mr. Swindell was not inaptly named. He had started life as a cleaner of railway engines but his natural abilities brought him far from that employment. He was at this time known as 'The Napoleon of the Turf' or 'Lord Freddy', sobriquets which he greatly enjoyed. It was he who, on being asked by a friend what he should do having been paid twice over by mistake, made the immortal answer: 'Do, lad? Look hard at him and the next time thee meets him perhaps he'll pay thee a third time!'

Swindell had a good colt, Tomahawk, and he was in the Lincoln with 6 st. 4 lb. His natural acuteness had already made him mark down Archer as the best lightweight he could get. He sent the colt to Dawson to train indicating that he wanted Archer to ride him. In the race Archer did everything right and won much as he liked. Mr. Swindell took an immense amount of money out of the ring and expressed his pleasure with a substantial present. It was a good beginning to the season. Better was to follow.

Dawson had in his care a four-year-old of Lord Falmouth's called Andred. By Blair Athol, Andred was, like many of that sire's stock, something of a queer customer and he would not go for every jockey. Ridden by Fordham then known as 'the Demon' and reigning supreme as the most skilled jockey on the Turf Andred ran unplaced in the Lincoln and again in the City and Suburban. Next time out, in the Great Cheshire Stakes, Archer was given the ride and won on him carrying 8 st. 2 lb. After that Andred was entered in the Ditch Mile Handicap at the Newmarket Spring Meeting and set to carry 9 st. 3 lb. Archer again had the ride—with no less than 3 st. of lead under him.

The jockeys of those days regarded the Ditch Mile as a very severe and testing course. Both Custance and Fordham, who were the two most experienced riders of their day, were of the opinion that it took more getting than the Rowley Mile. In this race Custance rode King Lud, a useful horse of Lord Lonsdale's, who had insisted on running him against the wishes of his astute trainer Captain Machell who wanted him put by for another and easier day. Custance was a very strong jockey who had ridden innumerable winners for Mat Dawson when he trained for Mr. Merry some years earlier.

About two hundred yards from home Custance, thinking Archer was taking things too easily on Andred, set King Lud alight and got first run on him. In a desperate finish King Lud just got home by a neck.

Custance blamed Archer and Archer blamed himself for losing that race. In fact, giving away 7 lb. and having to nurse Andred for one effort and one only, Archer did exceptionally well to make such a race of it. Knowing Andred as they did both Lord Falmouth and Mat Dawson found more to praise than to blame in his riding of the horse. Andred had made fools of more experienced jockeys than him. He got the mount on Atlantic in the Two Thousand Guineas.

Atlantic had not been easy to train and neither Dawson nor Lord Falmouth fancied him. The fact that he did not think he had got Atlantic quite straight in condition is said to have influenced Dawson in letting Archer ride him. Certainly there was very little of either money or confidence from the stable behind the colt who started at 10-1. Again, with almost 3 st. in lead underneath him, Archer rode a copybook race, holding Atlantic up for one perfectly timed effort and then producing him with one of his determined, driving finishes to get him home by a neck.

His first two-year-old winner came that year also at Epsom on Lord Falmouth's Ladylove. Indeed winner after winner continued to come in.

But as yet Dawson and Lord Falmouth had made no decision about their retainer. Archer did not, for instance, ride Atlantic in either the Derby or the St. Leger. He had his first ride in the Derby that year on Mr. Johnstone's King of Tyne and was unplaced. But he continued to ride Andred who quite obviously went better for him than for anyone else. More and more winners came along and every day that passed there were more owners searching for his services. His feet were on the ladder but he had not yet reached where he wanted to be—the very top. And another setback was in store.

Frederick Swindell for whom Archer had won the Lincoln had his eye on another big handicap and another coup. He had entered a four-year-old gelding of his by Wamba and out of Truth, known as the Truth Gelding—horses could then run unnamed—for the Cesarewitch. The Truth Gelding had run unsuccessfully in minor races as a two-year-old when trained by Scott and had not been out since. Mr. Swindell, however, knew he was useful. He took him away from Scott and sent him to Mat Dawson with instructions to try him quietly and in secret. The trial was convincing and Swindell made sure that Archer would be free to ride him for in view of the gelding's lack of public form he felt certain of getting into the handicap with a very low weight.

Admiral Rous, then eighty years of age was puzzled by the entry of the Truth Gelding. No one knew better than he the machinations of Mr. Swindell. He felt sure there was a plot of some sort afoot but what weight to give the gelding he could not determine.

Meeting George Hodgman, a bookmaker and betting man at Leamington one evening in September after racing and knowing him to be a friend of Swindell's he asked him if he knew anything about the gelding. The old Admiral confessed that he had nothing to go on since the gelding had not run for two years. He then produced his draft handicap and showed it to Hodgman. This was not unusual, for Hodgman and he often prepared handicaps together. The gelding was down at all sorts of weights ranging from 5 st. 12 lb. to 7 st. 4 lb.

Hodgman mentioned that he was having a drink later on that evening with Swindell and some of his friends. It was indeed a sign of the Admiral's failing powers that he asked Hodgman to find out from Swindell if he fancied his chances.

'You really don't expect that that old fox would tell me anything?' Hodgman said, but he carried out the Admiral's request just the same.

'Tell him,' Swindell said, 'that if he's got six stone on him he may scratch the d——d horse. And, further, tell him he can have the brute for a hundred.'

'Say two hundred, Fred,' remarked one of the boon companions. 'The old boy might take you at your word and give a hundred.'

Hodgman conveyed the first part of the conversation but not the second to the Admiral who made up his mind to put the Truth Gelding in at 5 st. 12 lb.

When Mr. Swindell heard the news he rejoiced. He also prudently kept out of Hodgman's way for he knew that Hodgman, having carried the message, felt that if anything was going on he should be in on it. By the day of the race Swindell had backed the Truth Gelding to win him £100,000 and both Hodgman and the Admiral, learning this, were highly indignant, especially the

[32]

Admiral who had been properly fooled. As well as that he had lost his market. In those days both officials and jockeys were allowed to bet and once his handicap had been published the Admiral would accommodate anybody. He went to Mat Dawson about the matter and Dawson told him bluntly that the gelding was a certainty at the weights. So, on all counts, he should have been.

But, unrealized by any of them and not taken into account at all, was the fact that Archer, as boys will, had suddenly that summer shot up to his full height of 5 ft. 8½ in., and that with the increase in height had come muscle, bone—and weight. When October came round he could no longer do six stone or anything like it. So he had to waste. Thus began the dreadful routine of starvation diet, Turkish baths and purgatives. The seeds of the ultimate tragedy were sown that year.

Despite the drastic régime to which he subjected himself Archer could still not do the weight. He weighed out at 6 st. 1 lb.—three pounds overweight. The wasting and the weakness it brought with it caused the downfall of the great coup. As ever he did not give in without a fight and he was only beaten a neck by Lord Ailesbury's Adventurière, ridden by Glover a very strong lightweight jockey. But ever afterwards he maintained that the wasting beat him, that his strength ran out and he should have won. He was right.

Archer's reputation, however, was now such that only his self-esteem suffered from this defeat. He went on to head the list of winning riders with 147 wins and to become champion jockey for the first time.

Dawson and Lord Falmouth took counsel together. It is said that Dawson stressed Archer's abilities and urged that he should become their jockey. Certainly Archer was now almost part of the Dawson household and a firm favourite with the childless couple. Dawson was not the man to allow his personal liking for the boy to outweigh his judgement but in this case liking and judgement coincided. Shortly after the season ended it was announced that the following year Archer would ride as first

c

jockey to Heath House and that Lord Falmouth had taken a first retainer on his services. The amount of the retainer was not disclosed but in fact it was £100 at which figure, at Archer's request, it remained for the rest of his life.

Thus was formed what was possibly the greatest winning partnership the Turf has ever known.

Now indeed the gates of opportunity were wide open. He could go home to his parents on his annual holiday with money in his pockets to help them and with everything set fair for the future, success, fame and happiness opening out before him—or so it seemed.

Chapter 3

Mat Dawson in 1875 had a crop of three-year-olds which was exceptional, even for Heath House. Most of the best of them were Lord Falmouth's. A believer in breeding from the mare rather than the sire Lord Falmouth had collected mares of known quality for his stud at Mereworth. Amongst them was his favourite, Queen Bertha, with whom he had won the Oaks and lost his bet on the St. Leger. A filly out of Queen Bertha had been a good two-year-old the season before and Archer had won on her as well as on Ladylove. She was entered for the One Thousand Guineas and the Oaks and Archer was to ride her.

But his weight had gone up alarmingly. The minimum at which he could now ride was just under seven stone and to do that he had to subject himself to a most rigorous starvation diet. His breakfast was a tablespoon of hot castor oil and half an orange, his lunch a sardine and a small glass of champagne. Mat Dawson had a Turkish bath put in at Heath House to sweat the horses but it was Archer who made most use of it.

He started the season as brilliantly as he had finished the last one, winning at Lincoln and Northampton and on the first ever day at Sandown Park which opened that year. He missed riding the winner of the Two Thousand Guineas, Camballo, trained by Mat Dawson for Mr. Vyner, for he was claimed by Lord Falmouth to ride Garterly Bell which was unplaced. But Spinaway gave him his second Classic by winning the One Thousand Guineas without being unduly troubled. Then he rode Lord

Falmouth's Repentance colt third in the Derby. After the Derby came the Oaks. Lord Falmouth ran Ladylove as well as Spinaway and neither he nor Mat Dawson could make up their minds which was the better. At that time the owner of two or more horses in the same race could declare to win with one or the other of them. Lord Falmouth refused to do so on this occasion though Archer was given or chose the ride on Spinaway. As a result of Lord Falmouth's failure to declare there was confusion in the betting, both fillies starting practically co-favourites at much the same price. Spinaway won but she had to be hard-driven to beat her stable companion, and she was to have two more hard races under Archer's hands before the season was over.

They ran her again in the Ascot Derby and she started favourite. But this race was to be the first of the long series of duels which Archer was to have with George Fordham in which by and large Archer was to come off second best.

Both men were superlative jockeys, each was almost the exact antithesis of the other and there was little love lost between them. Fordham was much the older of the two. He had been born at Cambridge in 1837, so that he was then thirty-seven years of age and had won almost every race of importance save the Derby. In an age of nicknames he was known as 'The Demon' or 'The Kid'.

Where Archer was tall and slim, Fordham was short and squat. Where Archer rode long with a graceful seat Fordham's leathers were short and his riding position, probably almost a foretaste of the present seat, was considered ugly; where Archer finished sitting forward, Fordham sat back. Archer was quiet-spoken and temperate; Fordham was rough-tongued and fond of the bottle. Fordham never trained, never took exercise save riding races, never was out of condition and never had trouble with his weight. Archer's riding life was a constant arduous routine of training and wasting. Fordham never knew what had happened in a race save where he had finished. One of the trainers who admired him and employed him whenever he could has said that after a race all you could get out of him was something like the following: 'Well, don't you see. I just went up and—er—don't you know, I—er—just managed to win.' Archer, however, knew everything that was going on and could retail it accurately afterwards. His intelligence was far superior to Fordham's.

But where Fordham excelled was in his superlative racemanship, which is the only word that can adequately describe his tactics.

Fordham was a coaxer not a driver. Archer had fine hands on a horse; Fordham had genius in his. It is the almost unanimous opinion of those racing people who have set down their memories of the times that Fordham, in every aspect of his art, was the more finished jockey than Archer. Certainly at Newmarket, where they rode innumerable matches against each other backed by the nobility and wealth of the day, Fordham was usually the master.

He had brought to such a fine pitch his concealment of what he was doing and how well—or badly—he was going that every jockey who rode against him confessed himself to have been well and truly tricked at one time or another. 'Fordham's kid' became famous throughout the racing world and earned him his nickname. By this manœuvre he won many races in which he should have been beaten. This trick would not work today, but races then were won run slowly and in snatches, the pace only being turned on somewhere in the straight when one or the other of the jockeys decided it was time to have a go and make for the post. About the time that someone would be expected to step up the pace Fordham would start clucking at his horse and apparently scrubbing him out but, under the persuasion of those superb hands, in reality not calling for any effort at all. Time and again jockeys, especially the inexperienced, would fall for the lure of 'Fordham's kid'. They would take out their whips and run their horses out too soon, only to have the mortification of seeing Fordham come later with a perfectly timed run and beat them on the post. This technique was exactly suited to matches

[37]

on the straight mile at Newmarket. He took a delight in fooling Archer. Sometimes he would tuck himself in behind Archer and the champion jockey's attempts to find out from in front what his rival was doing were almost comic. At other times he would appear to come with a rush where no rush was intended and baffle the other into making his effort at the wrong time. To such a pitch did he bring his ascendancy over the other on this course that on one occasion Archer came into the weighing-room in a furious temper, and threw his saddle at his valet, Solomon, saying: 'I can't beat that kidding bastard.'

But without question at Epsom and in the great races Archer was the master. The big occasion always brought out the best in him and his nerve was of iron—far stronger than Fordham's who, possibly because of his mode of life, entirely lacked Archer's dash and physical courage. Fordham, in fact, hated Epsom as did Custance who called the course both bad and dangerous and bitterly criticized Tattenham Corner which, far sharper then than it is now, was also sloped in towards the rails.

In this Ascot Derby Fordham was riding Gilbert, a horse which he knew wanted someone to make the running for him. In a typical deception he took him to the front at first and then, at the turn, fell back as if beaten. Archer on Spinaway went on and he and Earl of Dartrye commenced to battle it out at a rattling pace. This was exactly what Fordham wanted. With the others in front of him Gilbert caught hold of his bit and commenced to run on again. Fordham timed his effort to a nicety, pounced on the two leaders and won by three-quarters of a length—much to Archer's dismay.

Spinaway came out again for the Newmarket Oaks. Lord Falmouth and Dawson were still not in agreement which of the two was the better so Ladylove was allowed to oppose her. In fact Ladylove looked the winner until very near home when Archer really got to work on Spinaway and drove her up to win by a length. Spinaway had come in for one of Archer's severest punishments and when she retired to stud she was not really a success, whether for this reason or not, though she did produce one outstanding filly, Busybody, which Archer was also to ride, and which was to play a part in one of the crises of his career.

Victory after victory now came to him. Fordham might out-general him, Tom Cannon's extra polish and ultra light weight might beat him occasionally, but nothing could stop the steady stream of winners which flowed in at meetings all over the country, for he was an indefatigable traveller. Most of the winners were in the magpie jacket of Lord Falmouth but he would ride anything he thought had a chance anywhere, and at any meeting he could get to.

He had to win both to satisfy his own ambition and his parents' demands. Once he was a success these demands became all but insatiable. Always careless about money his father now openly lived on his famous son, and used his name to secure credit for himself and his family. The demands were met, the bills paid, but not a week passed without more and more of them coming in and only Archer knew the effort it took to discharge them.

It was about this time that he earned the sobriquet 'The tin-man', probably from Mat Dawson's joking reference to him as 'that damned long-legged, tin-scraping young devil'.

He needed the money. He had to have it to meet his obligations, which was why his eye was always fixed on financial advantage. Yet despite the stories which went round about his allegedly grasping nature, he was never a mean man. In fact he was always a soft touch to anyone in the racing world down in his mouth and with a hard luck story. The amounts he parted with to help brother jockeys who were having a hard time or gave away to the clever and greedy who knew how to play on his kindness will never be known. Lord Falmouth tried to help him, advising him over investments and practically compelling him to put away at least some of the large sums which were now coming into his hands. Amongst other things he bought land near Newmarket town including a holding adjoining Heath House. But the calls on his purse were heavy, and, despite what was said about him, he never really cared a lot about money as such. What he wanted was success and security, twin will o' the wisps that men, and especially men like him, have pursued for all time. As with many before and after him he found that one did not bring the other and neither necessarily brought with it happiness and peace of mind.

He was a compulsive gambler, and it was about this time that he started to bet heavily. This was permitted to jockeys in those days. Soon he was placing large sums on his fancies. Oddly enough his mother, at home, had caught the fever, too, and was betting frequently if not very heavily. He paid her losses. But whatever he had backed in a race he was never untrue to himself or to the owner for whom he was riding. The desire to win was always paramount. Lambton says that he knew him to ride some of his best races against his own money and tells of an occasion at Windsor when he was asked to ride a difficult horse called Westwood. Archer told the trainer he would but warned him he was having a big bet on another horse in the race. He mastered Westwood and got him up to beat his own fancy by a neck.

In this he was not an exception amongst the then leading jockeys. Fordham, Cannon, Custance and Constable all backed heavily and all were incorruptible. The same could not be said of some of the others and Wood, for instance, a very fine jockey then on his way up, was much inclined to adapt his riding to his betting. This was a course which led to a *cause célèbre* some years later which brought about Sir George Chetwynd's retirement from the Turf and in which Wood was almost flayed alive in the witness-box under one of the great Sir Charles Russell's most scathing cross-examinations.

He ended the season champion once again with 172 wins which besides the two classics on Spinaway included amongst others the Yorkshire Oaks also on Spinaway, the Chesterfield Stakes, the Clearwell Stakes, the Stewards Cup at Goodwood and the Liverpool Autumn Cup. He was still only eighteen years of age.

From the point of view of the Classics 1876 was a quiet season for Archer. None of them came his way although he won the first of his City and Suburban Handicaps on Thunder now sold by Mat Dawson to one of his new patrons Mr. Clare Vyner. This was a much more important race then than it is now and up to 1881 Archer almost farmed it winning it in all five times from six starts. His toll of winners went on mounting steadily and with them more and more offers of rides outside the stable came in. His ability, integrity and the recognized fact that even though he was known to bet heavily his owners' interests came before his own all helped to bring him acquaintanceship with the great racing personalities of the day. Two of these were Sir John Astley and Captain James Octavius Machell.

Both these gentlemen quite frankly lived on their wits, their knowledge of horseflesh and their ability to own and train winners and to back them when they won. Both men mixed in the upper reaches of Society. Sir John had been elected a member of the Jockey Club in 1868, and was a steward this year. Known everywhere as 'The Mate' he was a big, bluff, bearded baronet who, in his autobiography, captioned a picture of himself looking pensive: *clean broke and thinking it out.* Renowned as a wit two at least of his *mots* will stand up to cold print and bear repeating.

In 1874 he was elected a member of the House of Commons for the Northern Division of Wiltshire. During a campaign speech he rashly told his listeners that he was prepared to answer questions on any subject. Someone in the back of the hall got to his feet and asked him his opinion of Sir Wilfrid Lawson's Liquor Bill. Sir John had never heard of the bill but his wits, as usual, were equal to the occasion. 'I don't know much about Sir Wilfrid's Liquor Bill,' he answered. 'But I know that mine is a deuced sight too high this year!' On another occasion a form book, the forerunner of the present weekly publications, had recently been introduced. Going on to the racecourse Sir John saw a Junoesque woman clad in a very tightly fitting dress. 'Ah, form at a glance, I suppose,' he observed to her companion. He had been a noted runner in his youth and had made money backing himself in matches against various other athletes in some of which his tactics had not erred on the side of the scrupulous. He had also served with distinction with the Guards in the Crimea.

He was a hard gambler and a high liver. In the year 1882 alone he won £16,800 in bets and £15,871 in stakes and yet, to use his own words, was *cruel hard up*!

Captain Machell resembled the other in his manner of betting and mode of living though in very little else although he, too, had been a noted athlete and runner when a subaltern in a marching regiment, the 14th Foot, at the Curragh, in Ireland. The son of a Cumberland parson he had nothing beyond his pay and to keep himself going he would back himself in running matches and athletic feats one of which was to jump from the ante-room floor to the mantelpiece. With the money thus accumulated he bought racehorses many of which he rode himself in hurdles and steeplechases, and all of which he trained. Having exchanged into the 50th Foot he resigned from that regiment due to his commanding officer refusing him leave to attend Doncaster. He then came to England with a few horses. One of these was Bacchus who won the Newmarket October Handicap and an enormous sum in bets for him. He was thus fairly started. Henry Chaplin as a young man recognized his talents as a trainer of horses and a manager of a racing establishment. After Hermit's sensational Derby victory in 1867 Machell never looked back. His judgement of horses, races and men was acute and perceptive. Rich and aristocratic youths, taking their cue from Chaplin, when beginning their racing careers competed with each other in seeking to put their horses in his care. 'Captain Machell's young men' became famous, and none of them had reason to complain of the manner in which he furthered their fortunes on the Turf. 'Everything here on four legs is for sale,' he once told a visitor to his stables. 'But nothing here on two legs can be bought.' But he was far from being the popular favourite Astley was. Moody, suspicious, highly strung and hot-tempered, he had a biting tongue which he did little to curb. His verbal battles with the equally ready-tongued Duchess of Montrose have passed into history. But these were the cut-and-thrust of well-matched antagonists who recognized each other's steel. His acid remarks to others not so gifted in repartee lost him friends and patrons. When he informed 'Cat' Richardson, who had freely told friends and acquaintances of Reugny's chances at Liverpool that he 'didn't keep his horses for Lincolnshire farmers to bet on', he brought about an almighty row, the removal of his steeplechasers from Limber and Richardson's retirement from racing.

His excitable temperament, too, led him, in the words of his contemporaries, to 'burn the candle at both ends'. Richardson's sister has recounted in rather shocked tones how, going to the stable-yard to get their horses before an early morning trial, 'I could not help noticing how the Captain's hands shook even then, and it was a case of a glass of cognac administered by his valet before he could even mount and away with any degree of calmness or comfort.' But, she adds primly, 'On our ride to the course over which the trial was to be ridden nothing could exceed the Captain's urbanity, opening gates, and had I been a Queen riding beside him he could not have been more chivalrous.'

On the Tuesday of the Newmarket Craven Meeting of that year Astley, Machell and Lord Calthorpe, a patron of Machell's, were dining together. When Astley was well into his second bottle of champagne—the others were drinking claret—Machell suggested making a match, which was a favourite way in those times amongst gentlemen of the Turf of getting through dinner-table conversation. He proposed running his own horse, Oxonian, a good handicapper, against a three-year-old of Astley's, Brigg Boy, over a straight mile at Newmarket. The preliminary terms were soon agreed: the course to be the Ditch Mile, and a stake of £200. But when it came to the actual weight the horses were to carry an argument developed. Machell insisted on eight stone, saying he wanted Archer to ride his. He knew, as of course everyone in racing did, that Archer was having more and more difficulty with his weight. In the end Astley agreed, the papers were made up as required by the rules and sent off to Weatherby's. The match was to take place on the following Thursday. Astley's wits were not in the least fogged by the champagne which he afterwards said was the best he had ever drunk—and he spoke from experience. As he walked home he remembered that he had been told that Fordham was 'unwell' (this being the euphemism for one of the jockey's periodic drinking bouts), and was not riding, so that he would be unable to engage him for Brigg Boy as he had contemplated doing. He decided to steal a march on Machell and get hold of Archer first. Next morning he breakfasted early, mounted his cob and rode out to the Bury Hill gallops where he thought he was sure to find Archer. His guess was correct and Archer was there. Astley took the precaution of asking him if Machell had engaged him to ride. Finding that Archer was free he promptly booked him for the match. Archer then asked the name of the other horse. On hearing that it was Oxonian his face fell and he told Astley, 'I am afraid he will beat you, for I know the old horse is very well just now.' Astley merely confirmed the engagement and rode off chuckling. He was even more amused when, an hour or so later, he saw Machell setting out for the gallops and guessed his errand. What took place between Machell and Archer Astley confessed he didn't know and probably would not write down if he did, but that afternoon, as he was having a bet, Machell came up to him in no very good temper and said: 'You're a pretty fellow.'

'I thought so when I looked in the glass this morning,' replied Astley. 'And what good "pop" you gave me last night.'

'You have done me out of Archer and you know I insisted on eight stone so that I could have him ride mine.'

'Undoubtedly you were keen to have Archer; but I had a fancy that way, too, and I have got him—so it's odds on "pop" against claret for early rising, ain't it, if you only get it good and take enough of it?'

Captain Machell departed, bristling, for he had been fairly fooled and he did not care to have anyone win a trick from him.

The match on the following day proved to be an exciting set-to with Archer just getting Brigg Boy home to land Sir John's money by what he called a 'short neck' from Machell's horse which was ridden by Challoner.

The stake and the bets were Sir John's but Brigg Boy was a small and light-framed colt and he had received one of Archer's right royal hammerings. He never won for Sir John again and in the end, as he said himself, he was glad enough to get out of him to Lord Rosebery for a thousand.

It must be said that, despite Machell's suspicious temperament, he bore no ill-will towards Archer after this incident. He continued to ask him to ride whenever his other retainers allowed, but then Machell's aim and object, like Archer's, was to win races. His judgement and perception told him that Archer was the best instrument for this purpose available to him; he knew he was above suspicion and knew, too, that his advice and opinion on his own and other horses were of immense value. Machell's eye, like the jockey's, was fixed firmly on the main chance. Over the years a mutual respect for each other's brains and abilities grew up between them and they became firm friends.

Before the season was over Archer had his part to play in another sensational race. There were on the Turf at that time two brothers, both very shrewd, long-headed men called James and Sydney Smith. For some time they had been planning a gigantic coup with a horse of their own called Rosebery and had recognized in Archer the qualities of integrity, fearlessness and desire to win at any cost which made him the jockey exactly suited to their object.

Rosebery was by Speculum out of Ladylike and in 1876 had never won a race of any description. But the Smiths had tried him at home and in secret and had discovered him to be a stayer of exceptional quality. They entered him in the Cesarewitch and the Cambridgeshire in both of which, being a maiden, he was certain to be well-handicapped. Long before the date of the first race they approached Archer to ask him if he would ride Rosebery for them. To make certain of getting him they had to reveal what they knew—that in their opinion and they were both clever men of great experience on the Turf having originally been bookmakers—Rosebery was going to be a handicap certainty greater even than Salvanos. Archer accepted the ride and bound himself to secrecy.

Again the old Admiral was in a puzzle how to handicap one of Archer's mounts. In his original draft he gave Rosebery 5 st. 13 lb., but when he showed it to a friend he was told the horse might be a great deal better than he thought. On reconsideration he lifted Rosebery 18 lb. to 7 st. 3 lb. which was nine pounds under Archer's minimum weight. Thus his wasting had to be even more rigorous than usual, and he must have had some anxious moments when he remembered what had happened to the Truth Gelding in the same race.

Meanwhile the Smiths were backing Rosebery with every pound and penny they could lay their hands upon. What is more they were coupling him up to win the Cambridgeshire. And the horse was still a maiden.

Archer was pestered and, it is believed, even threatened, to give information about his unusual engagement to ride a maiden four-year-old in the greatest long distance handicap of the year, a horse, moreover, which was being steadily backed down from its original opening price of 50-1. He kept his own counsel and his mouth shut.

The excitement was made even greater by the fact that 'Lord Freddy' Swindell who had now bought a house in Berkeley Square near the Admiral's so as to keep an eye on the callers and draw his own conclusions, made no secret that he expected to win with Woodlands and was backing his opinion in his usual wholehearted way.

This time, unfortunately for 'Lord Freddy', on Archer's part there was no repetition of the Truth Gelding fiasco. He may have had to waste even more drastically than he did then but he was two years older with the additional strength and experience those two years at the top had given him.

When the watchers in the stands first saw the field Rosebery was in front. He beat off successive attempts to challenge him and won by four lengths. The men who worked the commission were standing by Sir George Chetwynd and he never forgot the shout of mingled triumph and relief which they gave when they saw Rosebery come storming home. The luckless 'Lord Freddy' was second again, and Admiral Rous came in for some more criticism which on this occasion at least was scarcely deserved.

More astonishing still Rosebery did win the Cambridgeshire, with a penalty of 14 lb. on his back, but this time, naturally enough, at a very short price. Constable rode him, Archer being claimed elsewhere. The Smiths made their fortunes and Archer had now proved in public that he could be trusted to keep a secret under pressure and to keep his head on a great occasion when huge sums were at stake and at risk.

He ended the season with the wonderful total of 207 wins, the first time he had passed the two hundred. He was no less than 132 in front of Constable, the second jockey on the list, who had only 74. There was plenty of money for the family now. They needed it and he saw that they got it. By this time he had set his father up as landlord of the Andoversford Hotel. During the winter months he stayed with his parents at Andoversford, making it his base for the sport he loved, foxhunting. He was still brilliant to hounds and cared not a bit about risking his valuable neck. In fact that winter and for several years afterwards he was often over at Captain Machell's helping him school his steeplechasers and hurdlers—a strange occupation indeed for the champion jockey on the flat.

Chapter 4

Early in 1877 he was back in his spartan quarters at Heath House preparing for the coming season. He still occupied one small room sparsely furnished and ornamented only with a few racing pictures and trophies. He lived with the family but he received no favours from Mat Dawson who treated him then and always, even when he made him a partner, as just another lad in the yard. There was no nonsense about Mathew Dawson. Success had not gone to his head and he took good care that it would not spoil his most promising pupil.

Archer accepted this unquestioningly. He knew what he owed to the Dawsons. They had his respect and devotion and, modest and retiring in his private life, he cared neither for the fickle plaudits of the crowd nor for the almost hysterical adulation he was beginning to inspire amongst some of the racing and general public. For his name now was becoming known outside the racing world. People recognized him in the London streets and pointed him out to each other, music-hall jokes were being made about him, his name was appearing in the general, as opposed to the racing, pages of the public prints.

This adulation continued to grow with the years until it came to the pitch where crowds gathered at his hotel waiting to catch a glimpse of him as he left. But it never turned his head. His natural qualities and the knowledge that to Dawson and his wife he remained a talented, attractive and very lucky boy, but no more, saw to that.

Mr. Robert Peck.   The Duchess of Manchester.   The Prince of Wales.   The Dowager Duchess of Montrose.
_ord Hastings.   Mat Dawson.   Captain Machell.   The Duke of Portland.   The Duke of Hamilton
      Lord Rosebery.   Mr. Tattersall.   The Marquis of Hartington.   Mr. Leopold de Rothschild.
Mr. Henry Chaplin.   Earl Spencer.   Fred Archer.   The Marquis of Londonderry.   Sir John Astley.
                    Mr. W. G. Craven.

3. Newmarket 1885

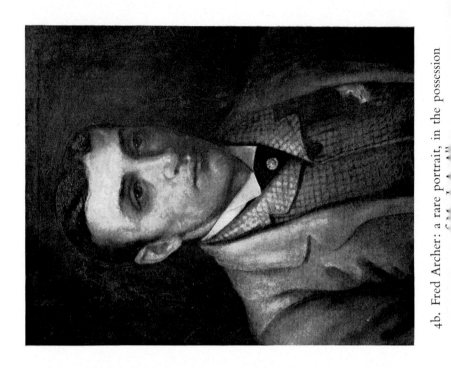

4b. Fred Archer: a rare portrait, in the possession

4a. The Duchess of Montrose

The next two years were the time when, as a champion, he really came into his own. They were the beginning of his supreme greatness. They were also the years that made the triumvirate of Falmouth, Dawson and Archer known all over England, when the magpie jacket was indeed a sight to be reckoned with on any racecourse and when the tally of great races won mounted to such an extent that Lord Rosebery had a printed card run off on which he could express his congratulations, thus saving him the business of writing letters as success followed success. In these two years Lord Falmouth won in stakes the staggering totals for those days of £30,000 in 1877 and £38,000 in 1878, almost all of it with horses ridden by Archer. No wonder he could and did say over and over again and in public so that all should know where the credit lay: 'I believe in Archer.'

Luck, as it must in racing when a series of great victories is run up and achieved, ran with them. Lord Falmouth was fortunate in 1877 in striking a year when the crop of three-year-olds was very much below average and accidents removed better fancied competitors. Archer for his part was lucky too, in that Fordham, his great rival, was off the course for all of 1877 and much of 1878.

The 'illness' to which Sir John Astley had referred proved to be prolonged. Drink, in fact, had caught up with Fordham and had him in its grip. He thought that his nerve was gone; he retired to Slough where he spent his days drinking great quantities of gin, with all thoughts of riding races again gone, apparently, for ever.

Apart from the absence of Fordham's brilliance as a competitor his disappearance from the Turf brought Archer into closer association with one of the cleverest men on the Turf of that time, or perhaps any other.

Educated at Harrow and the House Sir George Chetwynd had been elected as the youngest member of the Jockey Club in 1871. On Sir John Astley's term as a steward finishing in 1878 he nominated Sir George as his successor. Living on a princely scale with a large string of horses in training, Chetwynd had to rely entirely upon his knowledge of racing, his ability to place his horses to their best advantage and the prosecution of successful wagering upon which to support his way of life and the vast expenditure it entailed. This he was enabled to do for many years by a brain which was far superior to most of his fellows', an exceptional knowledge of men and horses, a mathematical study of form and chance and a complete absorption in and devotion to the business of horses and racing. He said himself that it took a lifetime to understand and master racing. Certainly he devoted his life and his talents to it. Yet he never quite mastered it; indeed, in the end, it mastered him.

Uncommonly handsome, reserved, arrogant and domineering, success had perhaps given him too much confidence in his ability to conjure profitable victories from moderate horses. Even then, in 1877, his integrity was to some degree open to question though he had not yet formed the alliance with Charles Wood, the jockey, which was to bring about his ultimate downfall. But there were many who disliked him and who looked on the running of his horses with a cold and hostile eye. When he superciliously chided a fellow-member of the Jockey Club for winning a race at long odds, beating the favourite and losing money for his backers he was quickly and curtly told that *his* horses when they started at the price didn't win. The implications of that remark were not lost on anyone who heard it.

He had a tremendous opinion of Fordham's abilities and when his money was down he was always anxious to have Fordham up. But in 1877 Fordham was off the Turf and Chetwynd was looking around for another jockey. In fact Wood rode for him the first time at Ascot that year but no permanent association was then formed between them. Archer had ridden for him on and off in the past and now he began to seek him out more often. It is significant that although Chetwynd had a freely expressed contempt for jockeys' tips he was prepared to listen to Archer and take heed of his opinion. That year, whenever he was free, Chetwynd had Archer ride for him. But Archer's commitments elsewhere were such that there could be no question of any sort of an agreement between the two. This, extraordinarily enough, played its part in the chain of events which brought Fordham back to racing.

For Archer was indeed being kept busy at Heath House. Silvio, a chestnut colt by Blair Athol, was the hope of the stable in the Classics. He had been a good two-year-old the previous season having won amongst other races the Ham Stakes at Goodwood and the Clearwell Stakes at Newmarket. Lord Falmouth and Dawson were believers in submitting their horses to fairly severe trials. Although Lord Falmouth did not bet he liked to see his horses run and he loved to watch them work in these trials at Newmarket. When Dawson had a three-year-old he thought might win him a Classic, it was his custom to try it at less than weight-for-age with a useful older horse over the Derby distance. So, early this year, he tried Silvio, carrying 7 st. 10 lb. against a four-year-old, Skylark, which had won six out of eleven races the year before and was set to carry 8 st. 7 lb. There were three other three-year-olds in the trial which started a quarter of a mile beyond the ditch gap and finished at the Rowley Mile stand. Silvio won easily by half a length. Huxtable, who rode him, told the owner and trainer that he hadn't wanted to press the colt and that he could have won by five lengths. This looked good enough to Dawson.

At first, however, the form at home did not appear to be working out in public. Silvio, ridden by Archer, was badly beaten in the Biennial Stakes by a very ordinary horse, Greyfriar, though Archer put this down to the conditions, there being a storm blowing down the course into which the horses had had to race and Silvio hadn't liked it. But in the Two Thousand he was also well beaten, finishing a bad third to Chamant. After that confidence in his chances for the Derby faded to such an extent that he was allowed to start at eleven to one.

As well as many other races before the Derby Archer had won the City and Suburban once again, this time on Julius

Caesar who was the subject of a rumpus when someone tried to scratch him before the start by means of a false telegram.

William Archer and his wife came up to Epsom to watch their son ride in this Derby. In the event it was all plain sailing. Archer rode a clever race against what must have been fairly moderate opposition, using Silvio's reserves of speed to come with a well-timed run in the straight and beat Glen Arthur by half a length. It has often been since maintained that this was a lucky Derby for Heath House and that Chamant would have murdered Silvio had he not broken down in running. But a horse and jockey can do no more than win and this they had most handsomely done. What was even better for Archer than the winning of the great race was that his parents had been there to see him do it. Mrs. Archer was openly crying as she saw the welcome her son received from the crowd.

Now only the St. Leger remained to complete his tally of Classic wins. Mat Dawson also had never won this race. This year, since for one reason or another any horse which seemed to have pretensions at all to challenge Silvio went out as the days went by, it seemed a virtual certainty he would do it especially since Silvio confirmed his own form by winning the Ascot Derby. He started one of the hottest favourites for years at 13–8 against.

It was not to be such a certainty as they all thought. Dawson and Lord Falmouth ran a filly called Lady Golightly as their second string. She had been improving all the year and the amount of her improvement may have surprised them. In addition it was a very rough race and at one time Archer looked like getting shut in. But when it came to rough riding Archer was quick to give rather more than he got. He burst his way through a mêlée of horses at the turn, more or less by main strength and bad language. But he then had to ride his hardest to master Lady Golightly. Once he had done so the result was never in doubt. He won by three lengths, the filly being second. The Heath House stable and their young jockey had now won every Classic

[52]

in the calendar and Lord Falmouth's horses occupied the first two places in the St. Leger.

It has been said that Silvio was one of the worst and luckiest of Classic winners. It is true that none of the horses which he beat were of any great account save possibly Chamant whose injury finished his racing career. Rob Roy, for instance, the Derby favourite, was shortly afterwards given away as an officer's charger. Even Lady Golightly failed to make very much of a mark as a four-year-old though she did win the York Cup, and Silvio himself did not do very much afterwards though he paid Lord Falmouth handsomely for his keep for he was sold to France as a stallion for £7,000 where, incidentally, he was a success.

But William Allison, the first of the literate 'Special Commissioners', who, admittedly, was prejudiced in favour of Blair Athol blood, defends him, making the point, and it was a good one, that there was such an astounding wealth of talent coming on at Heath House at that time that, after his three-year-old days, Falmouth and Dawson were able to and did use Silvio as a trial horse. He was made to lead in their work two of the best racehorses Lord Falmouth ever owned, first Jannette and then Wheel of Fortune and this, Allison says, ruined him.

Jannette, a beautiful bay filly by Lord Clifden, was a two-year-old that season and, ridden always by Archer, she finished it undefeated.

Archer himself ended up by increasing his total of wins to 218 and was champion once again.

At the beginning of the next season Sir George Chetwynd was still looking for a jockey. Archer's established claims and retainers were alone sufficient to put him out of consideration. But Chetwynd had to have someone on whom he could rely. It says much for his belief in Fordham that he determined to see if anything could be done to wean him away from his drinking. He paid a visit to Slough, told the jockey that he was a fool to be behaving the way he was, and that he should come back and ride again.

'Me!' Fordham is said to have exclaimed. 'If I tried to sit on a horse now I should fall off!'

But Chetwynd and his friend Henry Woolcott persisted. Eventually they succeeded in convincing Fordham that he could and should return to riding and that there were plenty of opportunities waiting for him. Woolcott brought him away from Slough into his own home where he watched and helped him. Soon Fordham began to do early morning work on Sir George's two-year-olds. Tom Jennings, too, hearing what was going on, had him ride out his youngsters. His horsemanship had, of course, never left him. Gradually, living the strict routine of a training stable and denied access to drink, his confidence returned. He reappeared on the racecourse at the Newmarket Craven meeting on a horse called Pardon trained by Tom Jennings.

He was understandably reluctant to face the crowd. Custance, a merry little man who got on with everyone, arranged for him to be allowed to mount down the course on the way to the Ditch Mile starting post. His nerves came at him again when he got to the post and he told Custance that he wished he hadn't come back, that the other riders were only kids and that he didn't know any of them except Archer. And, as has been said, the antipathy between him and Archer was well known.

'Don't worry, George,' Custance reassured him. 'They'll know you soon enough when you get upside of them, especially at the finish.'

In the result Archer won that race with Fordham three lengths away, second. Fordham's riding puzzled Custance. He had not seemed to be finishing the way he used. He went to the other and asked him about it.

The race had brought Fordham's confidence completely back. He winked at Custance and said: 'You don't think I was going to let Archer beat me a neck the first time I rode, which he would just have done!'

Custance went to Jennings, told him what Fordham had said and asked him to run Pardon again. This was done in the

Bretby Plate and Fordham won with all his old strength and skill. The crowd rose and roared their appreciation of him as he returned to weigh in. He had come back all right. Whatever else Sir George Chetwynd did or did not do on or off the race-course the rescue of Fordham, in part dictated by self-interest though it may have been, must go down entirely to his credit. Fordham's second winner of the season was at Epsom on a horse of Sir George's called Calabria and again the crowd cheered him. Archer's old rival was back again and in his very best form.

But nothing, it seemed, could stop the triumphal progress of the triumvirate. It would be tedious to set down in detail the amazing list of victories that flowed in that year but some must be mentioned.

Having been second in the One Thousand Guineas, Jannette, ridden by Archer, won the Oaks and the St. Leger, the Park Hill Stakes, the Champion Stakes and the Newmarket Oaks. In the St. Leger Lord Falmouth had the first and second once more, the runner-up this time being his colt, Childeric. Meanwhile Wheel of Fortune, another lovely filly from Lord Falmouth's mare Queen Bertha, the best, without question, that she ever bred, was, like Jannette the year before, winning her two-year-old races with contemptuous ease. She was given, as were most of Mat Dawson's good horses, a considerable amount of racing which included being asked some pretty searching questions in handicaps and was only twice beaten.

Archer rode all these winners but he missed, for once, winning the City and Suburban. Amongst his other victories that year were the Royal Hunt Cup with Julius Caesar, the Champagne Stakes with Charibert, the Free Handicap with Lord Clive, the Wokingham Stakes, the Chesterfield Stakes, the York Cup with Lady Golightly, and Silvio won him the Jockey Club Cup. He ended up with the astounding total of 229 wins and Lord Falmouth's £38,000 in stakes, which has already been mentioned, was then a record.

It was once more said that luck was on their side. Pilgrimage, many thought, a filly of Captain Machell's which had beaten

Jannette in the One Thousand, would have beaten her again in the Oaks had she not broken down. It was thought, too, that there was nothing of any account in the Leger save the Heath House runners. That may have been so but there was bad luck as well as good and one personal tragedy, the first of many which were to darken Archer's short life.

In a moderate Derby Childeric, well fancied at Heath House, was beaten into third place behind Sefton and Insulaire. Afterwards Archer maintained that he was at least morally responsible for Sefton's victory. A furlong from home, knowing that he had no chance and seeing that Harry Constable on Sefton appeared to be taking things rather too easily, he shouted across to him: 'Look out, old Jim Goater's coming!' Constable started to ride again and got Mr. Stirling Crawfurd's colt home by half a length. Archer and Constable had always been friends, Constable being a lot at Heath House, but whether on this occasion Archer was proving his friendship or protecting his money it is impossible to say. Silvio, too, proved a disappointment and they had had nothing at all for the Two Thousand.

The tragedy was the death of his elder brother William. He died as a result of injuries he received from a fall at Cheltenham when riding in a £5 Selling Hurdle Race. William lived with his father and mother at Andoversford. A fatal accident had taken place outside the inn the day before racing and it is said that William had a premonition of his own death and did not want to take the mount. His father laughed at his fears and insisted on his riding. After the fall he never recovered consciousness and died the next day at a nearby house to which he had been taken.

The three brothers were close friends and Archer was desperately upset. Besides the shock and worry of this loss he was, all through the year, having really appalling trouble with his weight. Getting it down and keeping it down was made all the more difficult for him since he suffered from some congenital weakness in his feet. He was a bad walker and could scarcely run at all. This is one reason why he was rarely seen other than on horseback. Thus, sweating the weight off by runs, clad in layers of thick jerseys, the method adopted by many jockeys, was out of the question for him. Starvation, Turkish baths and purgatives provided the only answer. As to the latter he had now his doctor in Newmarket, Wright, put up a potion for him. This came to be known as 'Archer's mixture' and it was a devastating aperient. George Lambton tried it once when he was riding steeplechases and wanted to get weight off and said it was dynamite. Years later, after a rough crossing of the Irish Sea, Archer gave a friend a tablespoon as a pick-me-up. It was so effective that the friend could not go to the Curragh the next day. This was after a tablespoon—Archer took it by the glass. During the season the sight of food nauseated him. He is said once to have bolted from a hotel dining-room on seeing a steak and kidney pie brought to the table. In the winter, when he was hunting, his normal riding weight was about eleven stone. It will be seen what he had to get off to do the weights he rode at on the racecourse. How his physique stood the treatment he gave it as long as it did is a mystery.

However, when the season of 1878 ended, the worst years of wasting were still to come. He was now twenty-one years of age, he had been champion jockey for five seasons in which he had ridden 973 winners; he had won all the Classics and three of them, the Oaks, the One Thousand Guineas and the St. Leger twice. Although years of greater glory stretched ahead he was even then, on statistics alone, a champion of champions. It is time to take a closer look at him.

His height, as we know, was 5 ft. 8½ in. in his socks. He had very small hands and feet, a long narrow face which in repose—and it was seldom animated—had a slightly sad expression which attracted women of all kinds and classes to him. His eyes were blue-grey; cold, hard and calculating those who disliked him said: sombre but ready to light up on occasion, according to his friends. He had pronounced front teeth over which his lips did not quite meet. He stood with the stoop almost all tall jockeys acquire and the ridge of muscle across his shoulders thickened and grew with the years. He dressed soberly and very neatly, usually in a plain dark suit—'like a curate' one of his friends described him. 'He might be taken for a rising young clerk in a thriving bank,' wrote a reporter sent to interview him about this time. He took considerable pains with this neatness of dress. On the course his valet had to see to it that the colours given him to ride in were pressed and without crease, that his breeches were spotless and his boots shone like a mirror, or trouble followed.

At that time and for the rest of his life he remained utterly unassuming. He was happier with the old farmer friends of his Cotswold days or with his fellow jockeys than mixing with the great in Society or ducal houses. He made friends slowly and was not quick to give his affection to anyone. Only those whom he liked or respected, men drawn from the inner ring of racing either by knowledge or ability, were admitted to this intimacy. 'The swells' was how he dubbed the rich and titled who hung around him looking for information, ready to drop his name or utterances in conversation or hoping that some of his fame would rub off on to them. He despised these and, perhaps unfortunately for himself, was at times not slow to show it. He was quiet-spoken, retiring and utterly determined not to be lionized.

But once made his friendships lasted. Perhaps his great friend, Joe Davis, summed him up best. 'He was a man you liked to be with,' he said.

Mentally he was a worrier and, like many of his kind, he was a selfish man, self-absorbed and wrapped up in his own concerns. Care sat badly on his shoulders and the tragedies which were shortly to crowd thick and fast upon him came to one ill-constituted to stand up to them. He had, and was bedevilled by, a most unhappy combination of characteristics which, fortunately perhaps, is given only to a few. For he was that strange anomaly, the thinking, intelligent, hypersensitive human being who is at the same time driven by a desire for violent action and possessed by an all-consuming ambition. He was two men in one, the thinker, the worrier, the analyser, and the doer of great deeds. It was the first of these, galled by the unhappy combination of circumstances which befell him, that, tragically, killed the second.

Now that he was on top he had become far less severe on his horses. It was during this time that he had the rowels taken out of his spurs, and much later he told a reporter that it was then, too, that he realized it was bad policy to hurt a horse.

But if his treatment of his mounts was mellowing, his behaviour to other riders was not. Quiet-spoken and diffident on the ground, once on a racehorse he was transformed into a hard-swearing and vituperative man who didn't much care how he won so long as the race was his. He had the ruthlessness in action of the highly-strung. The racecourse was his battleground and he spared no one. The young and inexperienced could expect no quarter from him. Once a boy of Captain Machell's, riding a horse he had strict instructions not to expose, heard Archer say at the start: 'Come on, we'll have this young bugger over the rails,' and was so terrified he shot away from the post, kept up a strong gallop to get himself home and out of trouble as soon as possible and won by several lengths much to the Captain's fury and dismay. On another occasion he drove his horse against that of an inexperienced fellow rider he thought was going too well, shouting as he did so, 'You're not second, you can't object,' and when his brother Charlie, to whom he was devoted and who should have known better, tried to come up on his inside he had no hesitation in putting him over the rails.

But it was typical of him that, having given no quarter, he asked for none, either. After a particularly rough race in which he appeared to have got the worst of it, he was pressed to object. 'No, I can't, I started it,' was his reply. And there was one man whom he could neither frighten nor intimidate—George Fordham. He tried it on, once, the year Fordham came back. High words passed between them as they returned to the scales. 'You have taken a liberty with me, *Mister* Archer,' Fordham

[59]

said. 'And I will teach you to act differently. You must not take a liberty with George.'

Fordham waited for his chance. It came later on in the season. Archer was on Silvio, well-fancied and out for blood. Fordham made the running and waited for his rival. When Archer came at him, shouting, 'Pull out! pull out!' Fordham pulled out all right—slap across Archer. There was a bump and a lot of bad language and Silvio didn't win his race.

'I thought I saw some better going in the middle of the course and went for it,' Fordham said as he dismounted. He added, 'I don't think Archer will ever take a liberty with George again.' There was no objection.

In fairness to Archer it must be said that the dislike between himself and Fordham was not entirely engendered by him. Fordham was a conceited man, well aware of his own prowess and the reputation his skill in judgement of pace and unique methods of employing it had brought him. He did not at all like having this young rival stealing the limelight and setting up these amazing records. He did not take to Archer any more than Archer took to him and there is no doubt that there was a very definite amount of malice in the ways he found of torturing and deceiving Archer over the straight mile at Newmarket.

Chapter 5

In the early spring of 1879 Mat Dawson brought Lord Falmouth to Newmarket to watch a truly astounding trial. Four horses, all Falmouth's, were sent down to the Rowley Mile start. They were to cover the full distance carrying weight for age. These were the horses: Silvio, five years, already the winner of a Derby and St. Leger; Jannette, four years, last year's winner of the Oaks and St. Leger; Wheel of Fortune, three years, judged to be the most promising racehorse ever to carry Lord Falmouth's colours and whose prospects were about to be assessed; Charibert, three years, the least considered of the four but who was within a few weeks to add yet another Classic to the stable's successes. All of them were bred in the purple. Silvio, as we know, was by the Derby winner, Blair Athol, and out of Silverhair, Jannette was by the St. Leger winner Lord Clifden and Wheel of Fortune by Adventurer and out of Lord Falmouth's favourite mare Queen Bertha, while Charibert was by Thormanby, Mat Dawson's old friend which had won him his first Derby.

As the two men sat on their hacks and watched the horses go down past them, Mat Dawson turned to his owner. 'There's a sight my Lord,' he said, 'the like of which you may never see again.' It did not then seem to be an idle boast.

Wheel of Fortune won the trial without being extended. It was a wonderful pointer to what promised to be a season in which even the former triumphs of Heath House would be surpassed.

At first all went well for Archer and the stable.

At the Newmarket Craven Meeting he rode three winners on the first three days and four on the fourth. But he missed the ride on Parole, a tough American handicapper owned by the tobacco millionaire Pierre Lorillard. Lorillard was a friend of Jerome and Randolph Churchill's father-in-law and both were concerned with the establishment of racing in the United States, the forming of rules and the enforcement of them in that country. Under their influence racing was well-maintained and strictly run. He had also had considerable success as an owner. As success came so his thoughts began to turn eastward. This year, as a start, he sent to England a small string under the care of a Mr. Robins, the actual training being done by a man called Pincus.

Robins had an introduction to Sir John Astley and made use of it. Sir John entertained his visitor in the usual way and was invited to come and see the string work. He was impressed by their looks with the exception of the lead horse which he described as a 'rough-coated old gelding'. This was Parole.

Despite Robins' open assurances that Parole was more than useful Sir John, in his usual way, would have none of him. Robins insisted that Parole would win the Newmarket Handicap. Sir John had his own horse, Drumhead, in the same race. He was getting 1 st. 2 lb. from Parole and he would not hear of defeat. Again, as was his way, he went into the ring and backed his horse according to his beliefs. Archer knew better than Sir John for he had guessed Parole's quality. He wanted to ride him and Pincus wanted him to ride but the claims of other owners prevailed and Archer had the mortification of seeing Parole get up on the post to beat the great Isonomy. This defeat caused a great deal of consternation, not least to Sir John. 'You can't go by looks, that's for certain, ain't it?' was his rueful comment.

But Isonomy had won last year's Cambridgeshire and was generally held to have been about the best three-year-old in training and likely to have won at least one Classic had he been started. Needless to say Archer filed away the result of this race in his head for future reference.

Isonomy was owned by Mr. Fred Gretton, a rich brewer and a heavy gambler, and trained for him by John Porter of Kingsclere. A quiet unassuming man who had been a very bad jockey before he became a very good trainer, Porter shared with Mat Dawson pre-eminence in their profession during that era. By the time he retired from the Turf he had trained the winners of no less than seven Derbys. Great names including, a few years later, that of H.R.H. the Prince of Wales, thronged the stable. Beneath his mild exterior he was tough and dictatorial. Owners did what he wanted or else took their horses elsewhere. A great believer in giving his horses time, the year before he had determined that Isonomy, a small, light-framed colt, should get it and not be subjected to punishment in the Classics. Fortunately this fell in with Mr. Gretton's schemes for hitting the ring. His only race was the Cambridgeshire. An unknown quantity, for his abilities had been kept secret from the touts, he was allowed to start at 40–1. He slammed a field of no less than thirty-eight runners and Mr. Gretton came away with £40,000 in his pocket. The horse was then put by until the following season and, although an expensive disappointment to his connections in the Newmarket Handicap Archer and Heath House were to discover just how good he was before the season was over.

Archer made certain of getting the future rides on Parole and with him he won the City and Suburban once again, and then the Great Metropolitan. Truly the season was beginning well.

After that came the Two Thousand Guineas. Probably because whispers were circulating as to his wind Charibert was allowed to start at the price of 25–1, extraordinary indeed for a horse of Lord Falmouth's trained by Mat Dawson and ridden by Archer. In the event he won comfortably enough; Archer followed this by massacring a moderate field on Wheel of Fortune in the One Thousand and went on to do the same to a rather better one in the Oaks. So, three out of the five Classics were that season added to the growing score. Wheel of Fortune was

[63]

immediately made a raging favourite for the St. Leger and looked upon as a virtual certainty. It was a wonderful beginning and appeared to bear out the golden prospects engendered by the great trial. Then things began to go wrong.

The whispers about Charibert's wind had been well-founded and the trouble became rapidly worse. Much more serious still was the fact that Wheel of Fortune's legs began to give Mat Dawson reason to think she might not stand up to a full St. Leger preparation. Silvio, too, which had been kept for Cup races and handicaps, was failing to win them possibly because, as Allison suggests, too much use of him was being made in trials at home, possibly because he had gone up in the weights and, as those less prejudiced than Allison suggested, like others of his breed, he did not really relish a struggle. He was beaten, giving weight away to good horses in two important races, the Gold Vase at Ascot by Isonomy and the Hardwicke Stakes by Chippendale who was receiving no less than 18 lb. and who went on to win the Cesarewitch. In the Hardwicke Stakes odds of 6-4 were laid on him and Archer was blamed in certain quarters for riding a bad race. It is much more probable that no one but Archer could have given Silvio the easy he wanted at the right time and come again at exactly the right moment to be beaten by only a head with that burden on his back. In the Banbury Stakes at the Newmarket July meeting Silvio took on a good French horse, Phénix. After his defeats he was now receiving 5 lb. and odds were laid on the other. Entirely due to Archer Silvio lost nothing in defeat but the race. After a desperate battle for a hundred yards out he was only beaten a head. Archer's mixture of brains, cajolery and ruthless application of strength were again alone responsible for getting a horse, who was now showing clear signs of a distaste for racing, so near to the winner.

'He is a wonder,' the Duke of Beaufort wrote about him during that time. 'He establishes a feeling, an affinity, or something of that sort, between himself and his horse and he makes some of them gallop when no other living man could do so.'

5. Fred Archer on Ormonde by Emil Adam

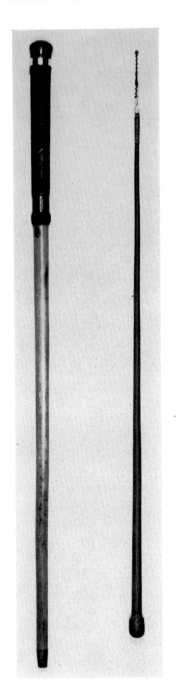

Heath Lanee
Newmarket
Jan¹⁰ 10ᵗʰ 1881

Dear Sir,

In reply to yours of the
6ᵗʰ, I beg to say that I have
ridden the winner of a
Galloway Steeplechase at
Bangor, but never rode a
winner of a hurdlerace

I remain
Yours truly
F. Archer.

6a. Fred Archer's Walking Stick and Whip
6b. Fred Archer—the last photograph. Taken in Dublin
6c. Fred Archer's letter dated January 10th 1881 (almost certainly
written for him by Davis)

Silvio's defeats were a blow to the stable, but worse was to follow. With odds of 6–4 laid on her Wheel of Fortune won the Prince of Wales's Stakes at Ascot in a canter. She was then sent to York for the Yorkshire Oaks, her final race before the St. Leger. It is said that two days before the race Mat Dawson found an enlargement in one of her forelegs below the fetlock and became convinced that whatever happened, whether she ran at York or not, she would not stand training for the St. Leger. A consultation was held between himself, Falmouth and Archer where it was decided in view of the very moderate opposition to let her take her chance in the race. She won without ever being asked to race and appearing to pull Archer almost out of the saddle all the way.

So easy was her victory that they ran her again two days later in the Great Yorkshire Stakes. Receiving 3 lb. from Adventurer and with odds of 3–1 laid on her she was beaten. After the race it was found that she had indeed broken down and she was taken out of all her engagements including the St. Leger.

She was a resplendent mare, beautiful and gracious. She had staying power combined with speed and courage. She was the best racehorse Lord Falmouth ever owned and she never had a real opportunity of proving how great she was. Archer always had a tremendous affection for her. Once, in an interview, he said that she and St. Simon were the best he had ridden and when afterwards on the many occasions he was asked to name the finest horses with which he had been associated he would never leave her out. 'Don't forget the mare,' he would say. 'She was wonderfully good.'

To make matters even worse for Heath House, Charibert had now gone so badly wrong that Lord Falmouth sold him for a pittance to Mr. Clare Vyner. So, since Silvio had finished with racing and retired to stud, out of that wonderful wealth of talent in the spring trial only Jannette was left.

Jannette had been another disappointment. She had been trained for the Ascot Gold Cup and had been beaten out of sight by Isonomy. In fact she had not won a single important race. She was entered in the Doncaster Cup but so was Isonomy and Dawson was in some doubt whether it was worth while running her.

The only horse owned by Lord Falmouth and trained by Mat Dawson to compete for the St. Leger this year was Muley Edris, an in-and-out runner and a bad-tempered, savage brute. Archer did not ride him in that St. Leger, Lord Rosebery having asked him to ride Visconti which had been third in the Derby and Lord Falmouth had agreed to release him. But it was Archer who had tamed Muley Edris. As a two-year-old Muley Edris was vicious, difficult and intractable. Although Archer's methods had mellowed he was never at any time one to leave a horse, however bad-tempered or unmanageable, in any doubt as to who was the master. He had given Muley Edris some unmerciful hammerings, had got him on to the racecourse and, what was more, had won on him. But the horse had fought against Archer at the start and tried to pack it in at the finish. For both of these efforts he had received a punishment he was unlikely to forget. In fact he did not forget with results which were almost fatal to Archer's life and his career.

But that was in the future. At the moment, at Doncaster, Archer was down the field in the St. Leger and badly beaten on Jannette in the Queen's Plate. It seemed to everyone that there was nothing to oppose Isonomy in the Cup with any sort of a chance and there was even talk of a walkover. Falmouth and Dawson, however, smarting under their wounds, decided to put Archer up on Jannette and at least make the favourite run for his money.

It was thought that this could only be a gesture and no one expected very much from a race in which odds of no less than 7–1 were laid on Isonomy.

Tom Cannon was engaged to ride the favourite. He was a slight man and a gentle jockey, the descendant of a long line of horsemen. He rarely hit a horse and never punished one, relying on winning his races by the persuasion contained in his superb and delicate hands, his outstanding judgement of pace and the perfection of his timing. Though he admired him, Archer sometimes referred to him as a 'pretty' jockey which, as with most of Archer's reflections on racing, fairly summed him up. He was no weakling, however, and could hold his own with the best. Along with Archer and Fordham he was generally considered to be head and shoulders above the rest of the jockeys then riding.

Porter put in a horse called Monk as a pacemaker for Isonomy, Lord Durham ran Glendale and these were the only other starters.

Glendale never got into the race at all and Monk was soon done with. The watchers and those who had backed him then expected Isonomy to come clear away and win his race with ease. To their surprise and dismay they saw that Jannette was hanging on to the favourite. Indeed, to some of those on the stands she appeared to be going the better of the two. The dismay became worse when it was seen that Cannon had begun to ride and still was not shaking Archer off. At the distance Jannette closed on the favourite and the two really started to race.

They were right on top of each other with Isonomy on the inside. So far as anyone could tell neither had the advantage. On the stands Sir John Astley was expressing his feelings in pungent and penetrating tones. He had laid the odds to thousands and was inclined to talk very loudly indeed through his pocket when his money appeared to be in danger—as it was now.

The two horses were virtually locked together. There can be no doubt that Archer was lying against Cannon and squeezing him on to the rails. Isonomy's courage and Cannon's skill just got them through the gap. They held on and won by a head.

On all known form Jannette should have been hopelessly outclassed. Again, it was only Archer who could have made the race of it that he did. But it had been, as many of Archer's races were, a very rough battle. One onlooker declared, whether it is true or not, that there was blood on Isonomy's offside shoulder from Archer's nearside spur. Certainly hard words flew between the two jockeys as they fought out the finish, and more passed between them when they returned to weigh in. The Duke of Portland has stated that Archer said owing to his weak ankles he could not keep his foot straight and that was how his spur went into Isonomy's shoulder!

Yet despite his roughness Archer was never disliked in the weighing-room, except possibly by Fordham. Partly this was because he could take hard knocks as well as give them and he never carried a quarrel off the course. Also, racing was a much tougher game then than now and much less strictly supervised. The give and take of bumping and boring was commonplace and occurred in almost every race though it must be said that Archer was more prone to use it and tougher at it than most. But this in turn brought about a sort of reluctant admiration from his contemporaries. He could do what they all did more effectively and ruthlessly than themselves. Major Dixon, the starter at York, tells how he once brought a friend down the course with him to watch the racing. The friend walked along to a point of vantage and saw, directly opposite where he was standing, Archer come right across the field to crash into a fancied horse ridden by Snowden, almost put him over the rails and knock him clean out of the race. Both Dixon and his friend came back certain that there would be an objection and a stewards' inquiry. Instead Snowden, riding in the horse, winked at Dixon and said to him: '*Ain't* he a hot 'un, governor!'

Partly, too, Archer was respected by his fellows because he kept his head on his shoulders and his feet on the ground. No one could ever accuse him of trying to exploit his success. He remained at all times and in his dealings with everyone, Press, public, peers, fellow-jockeys and racecourse hangers-on, his natural self. He never patronized, never put on airs, never tried to pose, never attempted to impress. In this he was favourably compared to his brother Charles. Very good-looking but quite unlike Fred in appearance Charles was much inclined to swagger. Colonel La Terrière states that it was commonly said at the time that the bigger celebrity Fred became the more side Charles put on.

Archer at all times stayed true to himself which is something men instinctively recognize and respect. Also he had, though it is certain that he never realized it or made conscious use of it, the ability to charm in whatever company he mixed. He was, too, brave beyond belief and this had always commanded admiration amongst men of action.

In addition his fellows admired and feared his superlative skill. Even those who had had their doubts about this, putting him down as a strong and ruthless jockey who had been lucky enough to land the retainer for the most powerful stable in England, were now revising their opinions. He was a master, Sir George Chetwynd says, of balancing his horses at the start and Custance, after years of experience as a starter, was later to write of him: 'I wish they were all Archers; if ever Archer was within two or three lengths of his horses you might drop the flag with the greatest of confidence.' It was alleged of him, as has been alleged of a more modern champion, that he had the starter bewitched, as it were, making him have eyes only for him, but this is not true, his secret lay in his horsemanship and the quickness of his reflexes.

But apart from the start which was, and is, of course, vital, it was now realized that he had finesse as well as power. His last big win of the season was on Master Kildare in the Liverpool Cup. Master Kildare had been beaten shortly before and was disregarded in the betting even though Archer rode him. But Archer had thought out a way of winning the race. He sprang him away from the start and went into an early lead of some ten lengths. The other jockeys were afraid of allowing him to get too far away from them, as he had known they would be, and they made use of their horses to keep in touch with him. Then Archer gave Master Kildare a breather, came with a perfectly timed run and won by a length and a half. No one else would have had the brains to conceive this plan or the ability to execute it. 'This race', Sir George Chetwynd wrote, 'was won entirely by Archer's cleverness in profiting by the start he was fortunate and keen enough to obtain, and by his tact in making skilful use of his advantage.'

After heading the list once again with 187 winning rides he went off for his winter's hunting. But that season he was going farther afield and into more fashionable places. After Christmas he was out with the Beaufort and on sufficiently intimate terms with the Master, the Duke, to ask him for the mount on Petronel in the Two Thousand Guineas. Much of his time was spent with Custance who had taken the George Hotel at Oakham, but he also stayed with Lord Wilton who mounted him when he hunted from Melton Mowbray. In fact almost every year after this he passed more and more of his winters as Lord Wilton's guest at Egerton Lodge. The widespread knowledge that he avoided the attentions of lion-hunters, kept away as much as he could from aristocratic houses and out of society, provoked comment on this association and, allied with his good looks, quiet manners and total lack of physical resemblance to William Archer his father, caused speculation as to his parentage. It must immediately be said that no evidence whatsoever has come to light to substantiate these whispers and rumours. Although it was unusual for Lord Wilton, 'The King of Melton' or 'the wicked earl' as he was variously called, to offer hospitality to a professional jockey, and even more unusual for Archer to accept it.

The Duke of Portland has gone on record as saying that Archer was one of the worst riders to hounds he ever saw. This is nonsense and reflects little credit on the Duke's knowledge of horsemanship. Custance and others better qualified to judge than Portland have testified to his brilliance across a country. Hunting reports from the shires in those days, listing the thrusters who saw the great hunts they then had, often included amongst the names of the noble and the bold 'Fred Archer, the jockey, who was well there'.

But, as on the racecourse, he did like to get on. The fast hunts across the grass of the galloping countries exactly suited his temperament, and he had little patience with those who got in his way or held him up. Once he jumped on top of the Master of the Quorn and, on being cursed, complained indignantly to Custance afterwards: 'I gave him a length and a half!' On another occasion he bumped a member of the field when jumping out of a lane with the result that they both came down. Naturally the other man was incensed and gave Archer a piece of his mind. He was only pacified by Custance coming up and telling him that Archer was not much of a rider, was over-horsed and couldn't manage his mount. The other had no connection with racing nor any conception who Archer was and when Custance prevailed upon Archer to apologize peace was fully restored. Next season, however, the victim kept an eye on Archer. Finding nothing to criticize he went up to Custance and said to him, 'Custance, I think that young friend of yours has very much improved in his riding since he was last here.'

It was at the end of this season, 1879, that Custance retired from the saddle. He had had great success and loved riding but he was not bedevilled by a highly-strung temperament, a demanding family and an all-consuming ambition. His reasons for ceasing to ride could be applied to Archer at any given moment in his career from that year onwards and are worthwhile setting down in full. This is what he says: '. . . it seems a pity that being blessed with a good health and a hard constitution, I should have been obliged to abandon a profession I was passionately fond of . . . I could get down to my weight in the spring easily in a fortnight and generally started at Lincoln; but to manage to remain so all the year was a fearful trial, and at the finish my doctor told me I must give it up or seriously injure my health, if the result was not worse. In reality I was trying to waste muscle instead of flesh, and every week it got harder and more difficult to get off. . . . It is the last pound or two that really takes getting off. No one knows, who has not been through it, the hard work it is.'

Archer was to go on doing all that and more for another seven years. It was no wonder his health suffered. If he had not allowed ambition to override discretion he would in all probability have lived to a ripe old age. But then he would not have been Archer. He belongs to history whereas few except students of the Turf now remember or have heard of Custance—if that matters.

Having retired, it is an indication of the regard in which Custance was held that he was immediately appointed official starter along with McGeorge. He spent the winter months at an inn he had taken in the Quorn country.

As he was later to do as starter, he exercised over the jockeys who hunted from his house a discipline which was kind and at the same time strict. He was constantly trying to temper Archer's thrusting methods with discretion and frequently Archer would tell him tall stories in order to shock him.

On one occasion when he came on from Egerton House Archer recounted to Custance how he had just had a splendid week—'Four days hunting, five falls, knocked two people over and was fined £1 and costs for riding on the footpath!' The following Monday he went off to hunt with the Quorn and on the Tuesday, meeting Custance's wife in Melton, said to her, 'Tell the governor I finished up well. I killed a horse yesterday!'

He had reason to enjoy himself that winter for things were moving more and more his way.

Robert Peck, who trained for the Duke of Westminster at Russley where Mat Dawson had once been, was one of Archer's few close friends. Peck was a shrewd trainer, a great judge of a horse with a wonderful knack of placing his charges in the right races at the right time. The season before he had had a two-year-old of the Duke's which he knew very well was something special. This was Bend Or. By Doncaster out of Rouge Rose Bend Or's very first appearance in the Chesterfield Stakes had been a winning one. On that occasion he had been ridden by Wood but Archer had been up when he won the Rous Memorial and the Princess of Wales's Stakes in a canter with odds of 5–2 and 2–1 laid on him. Archer, too, recognized his worth and his possibilities and he wanted to ride him in his three-year-old races.

Both men knew that the Classic prospects at Heath House for the coming year were not good. Peck was as anxious to have Archer ride Bend Or as Archer was to ride him. He urged the Duke to try to arrange some claim on Archer's services for the coming season. This was done and thus the scene had begun to be set for one of the most romantic of all Derbys and for an association in which Archer was to put upon the celebrated black and yellow colours a lustre which even they had not known before.

The then Duke of Westminster was a cold, distant, reserved man, one of the greatest interests of whose life was the science of breeding racehorses. From his Gothic palace at Eaton Hall he reigned over society in the west, keeping up his vast estates in almost feudal splendour, racing in the grand manner and universally believed to be the very richest of the ruling few.

In that year, 1880, another Ducal recruit was to come to Heath House. This was the young Duke of Portland whose name the skill of Dawson and Archer was also to write in bold letters across racing history. The name of Bentinck was, of course, one which had had a long association with the Turf, but the present Duke was fortunate in coming into the inheritance at all. His predecessor, an eccentric recluse who had extended his vast mansion at Welbeck by the building of passages and state-rooms under instead of above ground and then inhabited only one of them, was a distant kinsman. William John Arthur Charles James Cavendish-Bentinck at the time of his accession had been an ensign, and a comparatively poor one, in the Coldstream Guards. He had begun his military career in the Staffordshire Militia, had obtained a regular commission in the York and Lancs Regiment and had transferred from them to the Guards. In 1879 the old Duke's health was known to be failing and he was warned to hold himself in readiness for a call. He retired to bed one evening telling his soldier servant to call him with a brandy and soda, a practice, incidentally, not unusual in those days. The famous Yellow Earl of Lonsdale to the end of his long life breakfasted on a glass of brandy and half a bottle of white wine, and William Allison, not to be outdone by his betters, began his day on a bottle of Bass No. 1. When the servant appeared he addressed Bentinck as 'Your Grace'. On Bentinck's inquiring what he meant the servant said that he had heard in the canteen that an elderly relative had died and that, 'Your Grace is now the Duke of Portland.'

'If that is so,' the Duke is said to have replied. 'First drink that brandy-and-soda, then go and get me a pint bottle of Pommery.'

He immediately sent in his papers and took up residence at Welbeck. Racing had always interested him and it was inevitable that he should use some of the vast fortune now at his disposal to make his name known on the Turf. Archer rode his first winner for him at Newmarket in 1881.

Rosebery, too, was displaying more and more interest in Archer. Archibald Philip, fifth Earl of Rosebery, 'privilege in his bearing, distinction in his speech, largess in his hands', had come down of his own accord from Christ Church without a degree in 1869 because the authorities disapproved of his owning a racehorse. That racehorse, Ladas, that year ran last in the Derby. Racing, then and always, fascinated Rosebery. Yet all his life, despite his later triumphs which do not come within the scope of this book, on the Turf he remained something more of an outsider than an insider. Despite being elected to the Jockey Club in 1870 he knew very little of the technicalities of racing. A bad rider himself he was a poor judge of horses and indeed of men, on the racecourse if not elsewhere. He preferred the advice of jockeys to that of trainers which other and poorer men than him have found disastrous. In 1872 he lost £1,000 on the Doncaster week alone, and his most recent biographer says that his knowledge was never equal to his enthusiasm.

His resources were immense. Marrying in 1878 Hannah Rothschild the daughter and only child of Baron Meyer de Rothschild, the first Jew ever to be elected to the Jockey Club, his income increased from £30,000 a year before marriage to £140,000 after it. Although in racing, as in other walks of life, he wished for success, it was not altogether for success that he strove. Racing fascinated him. There was a raffish streak in his character which fulfilled itself and was allowed full play on the Turf. He loved the excitement, the gossip, the stimulation brought about by the grappling of wits and the exercise of judgement and courage at speed and on the stretch. This was something his staider political contemporaries could not and never did understand. Proud, touchy, unduly sensitive, Lord Balfour said that in politics Rosebery was made miserable twice a day—when the papers came in the morning and when they reappeared at night. Complex of nature, disliking criticism and hating defeat—'I am not aware Messrs. Weatherby pay for also rans,' was his acid reply to someone bold enough to congratulate him on being fourth in a big race—his character had some striking similarities with that of Archer. The jockey's ready intelligence, too, appealed to Rosebery's quick responses and fine brain. He liked to have Archer ride for him though his horses at this time were a moderate lot, he cultivated his company on the Turf and listened to his opinions with respect.

These men, along with Beaufort, for whom he was now beginning to ride more and more, were true patricians, unlike Astley, Machell and Chetwynd, the needy and knowing men of the Turf who had first seen and exploited Archer's quality. They had immense fortunes at their command, they inhabited palaces and were waited on by retinues inconceivable nowadays.

The eighteen-eighties were the high noon of Empire, privilege and aristocratic grandeur allied to immense power. These men lived indeed more like princes or oriental potentates than members of an aristocracy, their pomp and way of life being as great if not greater than that of the Royal Family. Portland's palace at Welbeck, for instance, was larger than Sandringham, his wealth far exceeded that of the Prince of Wales and he raced on a greater scale and much more successfully. They were the lords of creation and they knew it. However charming they were, and Rosebery within his lights was a considerate employer whom men were proud to serve, while Portland was in many ways a kindly and good-natured creature, they all had that in-built arrogance which comes with power and privilege on the grand scale. It was this that was to lead to the rift some years later between Portland and Archer.

Another noble owner, even if he was not quite in the patrician class of wealth and power of those described above, whose colours Archer was to carry with distinction in the greatest of races was the twentieth Lord Hastings of Melton Constable in Leicestershire. George Hastings, who should not be confused with 'Mad Harry' who squandered his fortunes betting and who was finally ruined by Hermit's Derby, was about the same age as Portland and a personal friend. He was yet another of Machell's young men and it was on Machell's advice that Master Kildare had been bought by him. Master Kildare was a five-year-old in 1880. A chestnut colt by Lord Ronald he had been third in the St. Leger of 1878; he had, as we know, won last year's Liverpool Autumn Cup, chiefly through Archer's brilliance, and was now set to give lumps of weight all round in the City and Suburban. It was generally held that he could not do it but Archer, as he was later this year to prove even more dramatically, had a way of making horses accomplish the impossible and he was a law unto himself round Epsom. Riding a finish which contained everything he had of strength, determination and will to win and which imparted those qualities to his mount, he just got Master Kildare up on the post. The second, Leoville, was receiving no less than two stone and the victory was greeted by a storm of cheering from the crowd. Hastings and his wife who, since her marriage, had also become passionately interested in racing, had good reason to be grateful to Archer for that race. A few years later he was to give them another and greater occasion for gratitude.

But 1880 is really Bend Or's year and it is therefore necessary to set down in some detail the extraordinary series of events concerning him and leading up to his Derby.

Because of the sensational objection which followed that Derby Bend Or has often been described. It is sufficient to say that he was a magnificent chestnut colt standing over sixteen hands, all of them quality, with an odd round black mark on his near quarter said to have been about the size of a tennis ball. He was a splendid example of the thoroughbred in every way, kind and gentle in the stable and the paddock, genuine and gallant on the racecourse. Robert Peck had owned his sire, Doncaster, for which he had paid £10,000; later he had persuaded the Duke of Westminster to give him the vast sum for those days of 14,000 guineas for the stallion. Peck believed Bend Or could win the Derby, vindicate his judgement and show that the money spent for the sire had not been thrown away. Naturally he wanted the best rider he could get, and that, in his judgement, was Archer. Lord Falmouth's runner, Apollo, was not of much account. He agreed to release Archer from his first claim. The engagement of Archer to ride Bend Or was accordingly announced to the Press as definite.

But on 1st May Archer rode work on Muley Edris. At the end of the gallop he got down to move some dolls. He put the reins over his arm; otherwise the colt was unattended. Muley Edris saw his opportunity and went for him. Those thrashings were now about to be repaid and with interest. Seizing Archer by the arm the colt got his teeth into the muscles, lifted him from the ground and commenced to carry him away. Then he dropped him and began to savage him. His knees were on the jockey's chest when, by a fortunate accident, his back legs slipped. He loosened his grip and almost fell over; and at that moment help arrived. The colt galloped away across the Heath.

Bruised and shaken, with his arm torn and mutilated by the horse's teeth, Archer was picked up and brought back to Heath House. His local doctor, J. S. Wright, was sent for and the wound dressed and bandaged. But the days went by and it did not heal.

Archer could not ride and was in continual pain and discomfort. He was in danger of losing his place in the jockeys' table and his income, save for the retainers, had ceased. Worst of all his weight was soaring up and the 26th May, the day of the Derby, was coming nearer and nearer.

Peck and the Duke of Westminster were, as might be imagined, seriously concerned. So was everyone at Heath House.

It was thought by many that Archer's career was finished. Even he could scarcely insist on continuing riding with only one good arm. There were no real signs of recovery in the other. His own state of mind can well be imagined. The thought of the career he loved being cut short by a senseless piece of savagery from a useless brute was torture to him. He fretted and fumed and did what he could to keep his weight under some control.

Then Lord Falmouth insisted that he consult his own doctor, the famous London surgeon, Sir James Paget. When Archer was shown into the great man's room he was told to take off his shirt and the wound examined. Sir James knew as little of racing and its personalities as Archer did of doctors and medicine. He treated and bound up the arm, told Archer to dress and as 'Thormanby', the racing writer, relates, said, 'Well, that ought to be all right in two or three weeks.'

'But shall I be fit for the Derby?' Archer asked him, expressing the thought that was never out of his mind.

'I think you can go.'

'Yes, but can I ride?'

'Better drive, my boy, better drive.'

'I fear, sir, you scarcely realize who I am!'

Sir James, in some perplexity, looked down at his pad. 'I see I have the honour of receiving a Mr. Archer——?'

'Well, Sir James, I think I must tell you that what you are in your profession, I am in mine.'

Immediately he appreciated the position Sir James became intensely interested and questioned Archer about his life and especially as to his financial loss if he were to miss riding Bend Or in the Derby. On hearing that it was likely to be in the region of £2,000 he said, 'You may well say that what I am in my profession you are in yours. I only wish mine were half as profitable!'

But, despite these attentions, the arm, though it showed signs of improvement, clearly was not healing quickly enough. With the depressive temperament of his kind Archer convinced himself that he was finished. He was in the depths of nervous despair. To try to combat this and get away for a while from the atmosphere of training and horses he went down to stay with his parents at Andoversford. This did not succeed in lightening his depression and one day he was complaining of his lot bitterly to a friend who suggested that he consult a bonesetter called Hutton. This he did and it is said that it was Hutton who finally put his arm on its way towards recovery. It is more probable that time, nature and his own physical fitness completed the cure. At all events he was soon able to ride out again and to begin to get his weight under better control. Some of the black depression dropped away. At least his career was not going to be finished. But whether he would have the full use of his arm by Derby day remained very doubtful. When the time came around it was clear that he would not.

Peck and the Duke were faced with an appallingly difficult decision. Arm or no arm Archer declared that he was fit to ride Bend Or and that he had the right to do so. Whether he could in fact do justice to the horse was something on which trainer and owner had to make up their minds. The decision was made even more difficult than usual this particular year since it was clear from the form that Bend Or was going to have to run for his life if he were to win and that a close and hard-fought finish could be expected.

There was one other colt of very high class indeed in the field. This was Mr. Charles Brewer's Robert the Devil trained by Manton who had a half share in him and who had engaged Tom Cannon to ride him. Unlike Bend Or, who was all quality, Robert the Devil was a big strong raking, bay colt with a hint of coarseness about him. Last year he had made his first appearance at Goodwood, winning the Rous Memorial very easily. His only other two-year-old race had also been a winning one. He was, as time was to show, a very good racehorse indeed.

[79]

Bend Or did not have a race before the Derby. He developed sore shins and, as with Archer's arm, they refused to respond properly to treatment. None the less, because of his two-year-old form, which was brilliant, and Peck's known opinion of him as one of the best he had ever had, he was made and stayed favourite for the race.

Archer was by now quite insistent that his arm had sufficiently recovered for him to ride. He himself was pretty sure that Bend Or would win and it was said that when Archer was confident he was, again as is the way with volatile characters such as his, very confident indeed. He had in this instance some reason to be despite his arm. He had ridden the colt as a two-year-old and in his work as a three-year-old and knew just how good he was; although he was not a conceited man he knew his own powers, and he knew how much he was worth to a horse over the Derby course. He wanted to write another classic win on to his record and he wanted, and needed, the money.

Peck and the Duke decided to allow him to ride. It says much for their confidence in him that they were prepared to rely on him to ride a very short-priced favourite in the greatest race of the year with an arm which they both knew was far from right whatever he himself said. Peck, too, had his own judgement and advice to vindicate, for the Duke of Westminster could be a difficult and ruthless master. Then Bend Or's shins became worse. Peck was treating them by rubbing in brandy right up to the day of the race. It was scarcely the sort of last minute preparation to steady anyone's pre-race nerves.

But Robert the Devil's connections were having their troubles, too. Tom Cannon was unexpectedly claimed to ride Mr. Gretton's Mariner. All the other leading jockeys were engaged so Manton had to replace Cannon with Rossiter who was never better than second rate. This may explain why Robert the Devil drifted in the betting and started only third favourite at the price of 7–1, though it was said that his owners backed him heavily even with Rossiter on him.

It was fortunate that Bend Or had the placid temperament of

the really great racehorse on the big occasion. If Archer had had to pick a horse to ride as the favourite in the greatest and most difficult flat race in the world with virtually only one arm he could not have chosen a more ideal mount. Nothing upset Bend Or: the tension of all those immediately concerned with him; the waiting, the parade; the long trip through the crowds to the start, had no effect on him at all. He remained as quiet and unconcerned as if he had been going out for an exercise gallop at home.

The same could not be said for his rider. Knowing the responsibility which rested upon him he was even more strung up than usual. He had had to get his weight down by a stone in the last few days before the race and had done it by a regimen of violent purgation and dosing with 'the mixture' that far exceeded even his usual extreme measures. 'I shall sit in the Turkish Bath and no doubt elsewhere,' he once told Dawson and Portland when, on another occasion he had to get weight off in a hurry. This is what he had done right up to Derby day and it had left him weak, nervy and irritable. His arm, though not as bad as has been sometimes said, was nevertheless all but useless and would certainly be of no help to him in a finish. It was not in a sling as many have described it but there was a pad in his palm and a piece of iron bound to the arm inside the jacket. Lunching off a crumb of a biscuit and a sip of champagne, testy with everyone who came near him during the morning, he was a mass of nerves when he was lifted into the saddle. Yet he did his best to conceal his anxiety, for Peck and the Duke were in an even worse state. He told them to remember Bend Or's placid temperament and rely on it and rode out on to the course to take his place in the parade. Nor did his nerves prevent him getting the inside at the start or keeping it when they got away. But from the moment the flag fell his pent-up tension exploded. He swore indiscriminately at everyone about him. Sulphurous warnings flew from him to give him room and leave him the rails or to take the consequences.

The race was run faster than usual in those days and Tattenham Corner was sharper then than it is now. Archer had reason to swear and cause for worry. Owing to his shins Bend Or's action was not right and he did not come down the hill at all well. He was in danger of losing his place and what is more he was being crowded. Yet he would yield the inside to nobody. At the turn the field was right on top of him, the air was thick with curses, and his were the loudest. He was so close to the rails that to get around at all he had to lift the nearer of his long legs on to Bend Or's withers. Thus began the legend that he rode his Derbys with one leg over the rails. It has been said of others since then but it was first said of him and it was Bend Or's Derby that began it.

Robert the Devil had opened up a long lead and in the straight he increased it. No one believed that he could be caught. The crowd were yelling him home and the bookmakers freely calling for ten to one on him.

Then Archer balanced Bend Or and began his run. The lack of an arm at this stage made little difference to his immense strength, his horsemanship and his ability to impart his own driving force to the horse. Bend Or responded to him with a courage equal to his own. The gap began to close. The cheering for Robert the Devil suddenly ceased and the bookmakers' voices fell away. Within the last furlong Bend Or was there with a chance but it was only that for the task he had been set appeared too great. A hundred yards from the post Archer, forgetting his useless arm, went for his whip and dropped it. But he wouldn't give in. Nor would his horse.

Then Rossiter, mesmerized perhaps by the thought of Archer behind him and the thunder of hooves bearing down on him, committed that most fatal of all errors. He looked around and, unbalanced, Robert the Devil faltered. Against Archer no one could afford the misjudgement even of an instant. In these last few seconds he saw his chance of victory and seized it. He called on Bend Or for one final effort. It seemed to the onlookers that his long legs almost lifted Bend Or level with the leader. Bend Or responded to him and stretched his stride. The two horses, locked together, came past the post.

No one could say with certainty which of them had won. Mr. Brewer was confident that Robert the Devil, who was on the far side, had won him the Derby. But up on the stands Sir John Astley, who had no very great opinion of Rossiter's riding, was assuring his friends that the jockey had thrown the race away.

For all concerned with either colt the minutes of waiting must have been anxious indeed. Then the numbers went up and it was seen that No. 7, Bend Or, was first in the frame. He had won by a head. A storm of cheering broke out which dwarfed into insignificance the ovation that had greeted Archer when he won the City and Suburban on Master Kildare.

As they returned to weigh in some of the crowd began to hiss and boo Rossiter. If Archer was sometimes despondent in defeat he was always generous in victory. He turned on them and shouted them down. 'It isn't true,' he said. 'The lad rode as well as any lad could, but met a better horse.' This was magnanimous indeed but it was also over-fair. For Archer won that race and Rossiter lost it, and Archer's remark to a reporter, 'It was not wise of him, perhaps, to turn round,' must rank as one of the racing understatements of all time. Had Tom Cannon been riding him Robert the Devil would almost certainly have won. Bend Or owes the fact that his name appears amongst the winners for the Derby to two things—his own courage and Archer's strength and opportunism. The feat of riding this superb finish without a whip and with the use of only one arm has never been equalled in the annals of race-riding and horsemanship. To make the achievement even greater they found after the race that Bend Or had spread a plate during it.

As if the race had not been sufficiently sensational in itself more was to follow. Almost immediately after the Derby rumours began to be heard that Bend Or's breeding had been wrongly given and the winner was not Bend Or at all but a colt by Doncaster out of Clemence. Mr. Brewer consulted Sir

George Chetwynd on the matter and subsequently lodged an objection. The hearing of this objection does not come within the scope of this book. Suffice it to say that after very lengthy and exhaustive inquiry the objection was overruled, but that doubts as to the correctness of this decision have always been expressed and continue to this day.

Archer followed this success by crossing to France and winning the Prix du Jockey Club, the French Derby, on M. Lefevre's Beauminet. Then his arm began to trouble him again and he had to stop riding for another spell. Fordham had the mount on Bend Or when he won the St. James's Palace Stakes at Ascot after a hard race with Mr. Gretton's Fernandez. There was, too, a very good two-year-old filly of Lord Falmouth's called Bal Gal who was to be beaten only once that year in nine races, whose finest victory he missed. In this she beat the American horse Iroquois by a head, and Iroquois and Archer were to make more history the following year.

Another of Lord Falmouth's colts, Charibert, despite his wind, had now turned into the champion sprinter and Archer missed other winning rides on him. So he had more cause for worry as his lead in the jockeys' table fell still further and the money he could have been making went elsewhere.

But at Goodwood he was back and riding like a fury to get ahead again and to make up for lost time. He won the Richmond Stakes and the Rous Memorial with Bal Gal; there were more winners at York with Bal Gal and others; then the St. Leger came along with Bend Or installed as a roaring favourite. Robert the Devil was to oppose him again and this time Tom Cannon was to ride him. The two stood almost alone in the betting, Bend Or being 11–8 on and Robert the Devil 4–1 against. Heavy rain turned the course into a quagmire. So bad was the weather that the parade was dispensed with and the jockeys were told that they would be allowed to weigh in two pounds overweight. It was a high class field, Beauminet, this time ridden by Fordham, being also a runner.

The story of the race is soon told. Bend Or could neither stay nor act in the heavy going. Robert the Devil was, however, suited by it, and his strength and action brought him home a winner by three lengths from Lord Rosebery's Cipolata ridden by Constable. Bend Or came in a very tired sixth with Beauminet just in front of him. Robert the Devil met Bend Or again at Newmarket and beat him a head, and later he again beat him by no less than ten lengths in the Champion Stakes. Archer maintained that Bend Or was the better horse and that if they met next year he would prove it. It is probable that not quite the best was seen of Bend Or that year and if so Archer undoubtedly knew it. He had had a very hard race in the Derby when suffering from sore shins and this, coupled with another close finish shortly afterwards when Fordham rode him at Ascot, probably left its mark for the rest of the season. But Robert the Devil was an uncommonly good horse and he showed it when he won the Cesarewitch giving the St. Leger second, Cipolata, the welter burden of 2 st.

Certainly horses in those days were asked questions no one would now dream of putting to them. To run second in the Derby, win the St. Leger and then the Cesarewitch and then two days later come out at weight for age against such a horse as Bend Or and beat him was a feat indeed. Whatever Archer said there is little doubt that, in 1880 at any rate, Robert the Devil was the better horse.

The interruptions and the disappointments brought the number of Archer's winnings down and also, of course, reduced his income. But he had not entirely wasted his time during his lay-off. For some years back he had been buying horses or shares in them of his own accord for jockeys were then allowed to own and race horses should they so wish. During this time he became even more closely associated with Captain Machell and acquired a share in some of his horses including Valour on whom the following year he was to ride what many thought to be the finest race of his career. He also became acquainted for the first time with the strange uncouth figure of George Alexander Baird.

Baird, son of a Scottish ironmaster who left him over three millions, was a tragedy of the times. His father had died when he was very young and he had no one to guide and help him when he came down from Cambridge to try his luck on the Turf. He was shy and diffident and very conscious of his humble origins. The ruling powers did nothing to lessen this consciousness. There seems to have been hostility to him from the first, which may have stemmed in part from his father's buying up of vast estates in Scotland from impoverished landowners. Baird had in him qualities of kindliness and generosity, but the social rebuffs he received drove him into the company of the riff-raff of the racetracks and they in turn preyed on him and accelerated his natural bent for dissipation. Also, his immense wealth and, at least at first, his success with women, provoked jealousy amongst certain of the nobility and gentry who enjoyed neither his financial resources nor his sexual prowess. His great ambition was to excel as a gentleman rider and in one respect at any rate he showed his good sense. Beginning his racing career this year, 1880, he decided to model himself on Archer. Standing about five foot ten he was much the same build as the jockey and he followed him from meeting to meeting studying his horsemanship and his methods. He also sought out his company and that of Tom Cannon on the racecourse and elsewhere asking for advice and help in the way to ride and win races. Thus by hard work and dedication he made himself into an outstanding amateur rider. He did once beat Archer and Wood in a terrific finish at Nottingham, and ever afterwards he maintained this to have been the proudest moment of his life. In 1880, aged nineteen, the faults which he was later to develop and which were to lead to his early death, had not yet become apparent. He was a shy, slim, diffident youth, bent, like many another on learning how to win races, and with the means and ability to do it. Like Archer he had trouble with his weight and breakfasted on weak tea and castor oil, like Archer he would travel vast distances to ride a winner at whatever meeting in however humble a race, like Archer he was popular with the public who knew that with

him they were always on a trier, like Archer, and in this he may
well have copied his model too closely for he had neither
Archer's charm nor his genius to get him out of the trouble he
got into, he was not too scrupulous about the methods he employed to win his races. At all events it was during this year that
the acquaintanceship between the two began, but Baird had a
long way to go before he approached his idol in results. He rode
six winners while Archer, despite the accident and the interruptions, rode 120, much less than usual but still enough to put him
at the head of the jockeys' table for yet another year.

Chapter 6

The following year, 1881, was one of the greatest in Archer's life. It commenced by Mat Dawson making him a partner in the training establishment of Heath House. He was twenty-four years of age. He had indeed come a long way from the nervous child of eleven who had presented himself to be indentured only thirteen years ago. Now he was a full-fledged partner in the strongest stable in the land, and when, that year, Dawson wished to extend his yard he had to buy the land from Archer on which to do so. Archer now owned racehorses either wholly or in shares with some of the names most renowned in racing England. Champion jockey for the past seven years, money in thousands was at his command. His retainers at about this time have been given as—first Lord Falmouth £100, the nominal sum which never varied, second Lord Hastings and the Duke of Portland jointly £2,000; third the Duke of Westminster £1,000 and fourth Lord Alington £500. These added to his presents and earnings and other minor claiming fees made his total income princely indeed. He is said to have told Sir James Paget that it was 'about £8,000', a year; the Duke of Portland put it between that figure and £10,000. In fact it was probably in excess of the latter figure though he always maintained that, being known to bet heavily, he lost large presents, for owners thought that he had already looked after himself in the market and reduced their presents accordingly. A year or two later when the Duchess of Montrose was definitely setting her cap at him she came forward with a huge sum for a fourth or fifth claim.

He was always attractive to women and, along with his professional and worldly success, their pursuit of him increased. He was clever at avoiding entanglements and yet at remaining on good terms with those who held temptation out to him. Dedicated to two things in life, winning races and making money, he had no intention of allowing thwarted wives, disappointed spinsters or predatory racing women to put complications in his way. Charming and courtier-like to all of them he restrained his relations with them to riding winners and, as he thought fit, helping them with their betting. But it was not always easy for in many cases this only made the pursuit by bored and high-born racing beauties all the more avid. His sister had told how she found in his bedroom a letter from a married woman 'of very high degree indeed asking why he was so cold to her and all that. . . .' Lady Hastings, who was herself far from being insensible to his charm, wrote of him long afterwards, 'The way in which some women ran after Archer was amazing. He was a marvellous man and a marvellous jockey. I should think there never was anyone a bit like him . . . and through all the flattery and absurdity of all those ridiculous women, his manners remained quite unspoilt—just perfection.' Bearing in mind that this letter was written by a daughter of Lord Suffield, wife of the twentieth Lord Hastings, about a professional jockey in the eighties it is in itself a revealing document.

His romance, if it can be called such, with the ageing Duchess of Montrose belongs to a later stage in his life when it really burgeoned, although already in this year when he was riding winners for her husband, she had set her eye upon him. There can be no doubt that she did fall in love with him with the ridiculous yet pathetic passion of an old woman for an attractive young man. She sought him out on the gallops and elsewhere and pursued him with invitations to her house and the theatre.

Rank, wealth, fashion and beauty were all at his feet—if he

wanted them. But there was one to whom he would always remain the same promising apprentice he had been years before. Although he had made him a partner Mat Dawson gave him no more privileges in the stable than he had done at the beginning. Archer had to attend evening stables like every other lad in the place and, what was more, he had to stand to attention when an owner spoke to him.

At the Newmarket Spring Meeting of that year he won his first race, the forerunner of many more, for the Duke of Portland. It was on a two-year-old called Marquesa. Portland was now buying horses on a considerable scale and taking an active interest in them and in the stable. He has told how during this time with a group of friends and acquaintances he was about to leave the yard one evening. The gate was not opened for them with the promptitude which Mat Dawson thought befitted their rank and station. The trainer turned on Archer who was standing by. 'Archer man, where are your manners? Are ye no going to open the gate?' he demanded. Archer, champion jockey, for years the earner of a princely income, friend of lords and stewards and nabobs of the Turf, ran to obey like a first season apprentice.

Yet another City and Suburban fell to him in this year. Classic horses in those days were entered in the big handicaps, given high weights and expected to carry them. Bend Or, whom Archer rode to victory, had nine stone on his back. He had to give no less than 2 st. 6 lb. to Foxhall, a high class American horse and he did it and beat him. We shall hear of Foxhall again.

Then came the business of deciding what he would ride in the Derby. Heath House had nothing of any great account and he was free to look about for the best he could get.

Mr. Lorillard was still racing in England and Pincus was still training for him. They had a useful, tough American colt called Iroquois which had won a few two-year-old races the year before. Pincus used old Parole as a lead horse for him and trained by the clock. This, together with his methods of galloping which were severe even by the standards of those days, were looked upon askance by the conservative English trainers. As with Parole, however, Archer's eye was able to perceive something of Iroquois' promise despite his trainer's methods.

But Robert Peck, too, had a very good colt in training. The Duchess of Westminster had died the previous year so the Duke's horses this season were being raced under the name of Mr. Grosvenor. One of them was Peregrine with whom Peck had every hope of repeating his Derby triumph of the year before. Archer having decided to ride Iroquois in the Two Thousand Guineas, Peck engaged Webb for Peregrine. Before the race he tried Peregrine with Bend Or at a difference of 16 lb. and Peregrine, a year younger, beat Bend Or with a fair amount of ease.

Peregrine won the Guineas from Iroquois, apparently unextended, and looked all over a ready-made winner of the Derby. But Pincus told Archer that he was perfectly satisfied with Iroquois whose training schedule had, he said, been held up and who could be made much fitter by Derby Day. Archer was not convinced by the American's arguments. Believing that Peregrine had the Derby at his mercy he went to Peck and asked him for the ride. Thinking that Archer had been retained for Iroquois Peck had already engaged Frank Webb.

'Give him a thousand then and put me up,' Archer said when Peck told him this.

Peck refused, saying that he must stand by his word. Archer went back to Pincus and offered him his services for Iroquois. Needless to say the offer was readily accepted and Pincus went on in his own peculiar way getting his colt ready for the great race.

The Derby was to be run on Wednesday, 1st June. The previous Saturday Peck once more tried Peregrine with Bend Or, this time at a difference of 20 lb. The result was a dead heat. Looking at what Bend Or had already accomplished that season Peck, who later declared Peregrine to be the best horse he ever put in a trial, knew he had something to bet on. But he still had

Archer to reckon with and, although he, along with almost everyone in racing, discounted the efficacy of the American's training, he knew, none better, what Archer meant to a horse, and especially at Epsom.

In fact Iroquois' tough constitution suited the strenuous preparation he was given and Pincus brought him to Epsom hard and fit and ready to run for his life. Although his wife travelled to see the race Mr. Lorillard was not there for he was helping to marry Morton Frewen, an English adventurer and eccentric, to Leonard Jerome's eldest daughter, Clara. Lorillard, his brother Leonard, and Frewen, spent the day in the Union Club beside the ticker, waiting for the result.

Peregrine was favourite at 6–5, with Iroquois, chiefly owing to the fact that Archer was riding him, second in the betting at 11–2. The start was late but Archer, as was usual, took up the inside position and kept it. As usual, too, he did not waste a yard of ground. He came round Tattenham Corner in the position he had practically made his own with the rails almost brushing his left foot. Webb had been wasting hard to do the weight and the effort had told on his strength. He swung wide on the corner. Just the same, when he balanced Peregrine and set him going he went so far clear that he was able to come across on to the rails. From the stands he looked all over a winner. But Archer, who had gone the shortest way, was sitting behind him, breathing down his neck and timing his run. Hearing the other closing on him Webb drew his whip. Again his lack of strength told. Peregrine rolled away from the rails. Against Archer to offer any such opening was to court disaster. In a flash he shot Iroquois into the gap and was on terms with the favourite. A desperate battle then took place between the two which ended in Archer getting Iroquois home by a neck. Well might Peck say, as indeed he did to a friend, that it would have been worth the thousand pounds to him to have stood Webb down.

This victory meant that Archer had ridden three out of the last five Derby winners. There can be little doubt, too, that in the last two years at least, it was the riding that did it and that he would have won on either the first or the second.

When the news came through on the tape to the Union Club in New York Frewen turned to Lorillard and said accusingly, 'The first American to win the Derby and you are not there to see it!' This did not prevent them celebrating the victory along with almost all New York, the whole night through. The first name the bride heard pass between her future husband and his best man as she entered the church next day was 'Iroquois'.

On the following Friday Bend Or and Robert the Devil ran their great match for the Epsom Cup over a distance of a mile and a half. It was the fifth and, as events turned out, the final meeting between the two horses and created far more excitement and interest than the Derby. It was also a meeting between two great jockeys for Tom Cannon was to ride Robert the Devil this time and there was immense speculation as to whether jockeyship could reverse last year's result over the same course and distance. They would each have a clear run and there could be no excuses for either of them.

There was also the clash of temperament in both horses and men—Bend Or placid and equable with his tall, determined, highly-strung, forceful jockey; Robert the Devil, inclined to the tearaway, excitable and edgy, ridden by the diminutive Cannon, cool, polished, skilful and relying on persuasion rather than power.

From the fall of the flag Cannon made all the use he could of his horse's greater staying power. He went to the front and stayed there, hoping Robert the Devil's strength and stride would gallop Bend Or into the ground. But this was Epsom where Archer was supreme. Again he did not give away a yard of ground, again he lay exactly the right distance behind Cannon, conserving his horse's strength, biding his time, waiting to unleash Bend Or's blinding burst of speed at exactly the right moment. He came to challenge just inside the distance. Neither horse would give an inch. Both ran straight and true under the whip. The stands rose and roared. Bend Or got his head in front and nothing Cannon could do could cut down that tiny lead. Archer knew exactly where he was and how fast he and the other were going. He won by a neck, with, it was generally agreed, something in hand.

Most people who watched the race were of the opinion that it was Archer's supreme confidence and judgement of pace which enabled him to cut the winning margin so fine but it must be said that Sir George Chetwynd, whose knowledge of racing and what went on behind the scenes in those days was unrivalled, has left it on record that Bend Or was not fit on the day and that Robert the Devil had leg trouble so that 'the race was no real test of merit'. If this were so then the narrowness of the victory reflects even greater credit on Archer's skill.

In the meantime events were materializing in the lives of two of Archer's old friends which were to lead to what many have said to be the greatest race of his life—his victory on Valour in the Manchester Cup.

For some little time back Sir John Astley had had his eye on a five-year-old by Hermit out of Lady Masham called Peter. As usual, however, with the game old baronet, funds were lacking. But when he won the Chester Cup with Windsor and landed one of his astronomical bets he found his account in credit again. A man called Gee had bought a colt called Peter at General Peel's dispersal sale and Sir John knew he was on the market at 6,000 guineas. His new-found prosperity was not quite strong enough to stand that price but he was determined to have the colt so he cheerfully borrowed £2,500 from a friend. Wiring Gee to meet him at Newmarket he there and then bought Peter for the price named. Jubilantly he declared that Peter was 'the best horse of his day or any other'. All Sir John's geese were swans and Peter was very far from being that. He had won the Middle Park Plate in 1878 and was much fancied for the Derby of the following year when his nomination became void owing to General Peel's death. He was a very good horse on his day but he was queer-tempered in the extreme and would only go for certain jockeys, of whom Archer was one. A more ill-judged purchase for such a whole-hearted plunger as Sir John can scarcely be imagined.

The day he bought him he sought Archer out and told him what he had done. Archer hardly shared Sir John's boundless enthusiasm but he agreed to ride Peter for him in the Hunt Cup at Ascot. Sir John assured Archer that Peter was a certainty, that he was bound to win 'whatever weight he has to carry' and went off to make another inspection of his new purchase.

The moment Peter came into his hands Sir John, whose enthusiasm could lead him at times to be both meddlesome and opinionated, began to take an active interest in his training. One morning, Peter having already done a strong gallop over a mile and a half, Astley spotted Sherrard who was then managing Mr. Keene's horses, out with his string, amongst whom was Foxhall. Sir John asked Sherrard to allow the two horses to go round the Limekilns together. Peter, giving Foxhall 2½ st., made mincemeat of him. Foxhall, as Sir John knew, was then being trained for and was well fancied to win the Grand Prix at Longchamps. Sir John thought and said that Peter could have given Foxhall another stone and beaten him. Flushed with this information he decided that Peter had the Manchester Cup at his mercy and that it would be a nice race to pick up on the way to Ascot. Wood, the stable jockey, could have the ride.

Captain Machell and Archer had a horse called Valour in which they were part owners, entered in the Manchester Cup. Valour was a useful handicapper but a mile was generally regarded as being his best distance and no one seriously thought of him as being able to stay the mile and six furlongs of the Cup.

At Kempton, a week before the race, as Archer was leaving the enclosure for the course, he handed Astley a note, saying as he did so, 'This will interest you, Sir John.'

Astley opened the note. It was from Machell to Archer and read: *if you will ride Valour in the Manchester Cup I will run him; if not I shall not send him to Manchester.*

After the race Archer approached Sir John and said to him:

[95]

'What answer shall I send the Captain?' and he then added: 'You know Peter won't go for Wood.'

Sir John was in a quandary. He wanted Archer to ride his horse, he knew Peter's peculiarities and that was why he had made sure of getting Archer for the Hunt Cup, knowing that Wood had prior claims in that race which ranked above his. On the other hand Wood had his retainer, there were no other claims on him for the Manchester Cup and so Wood had the right to ride. He told Archer that he could not possibly stand down his stable jockey and was then sufficiently ill-advised to add sarcastically words which he was afterwards bitterly to re-gret: 'Ride Valour by all means if you like,' he said, 'for all the chance he has of beating Peter at four pounds.' He then went off to start backing Peter for every penny he could lay his hands on.

It looked all right upon paper but Sir John could not get out of his mind the imponderables represented by Peter's pecu-liarities and Archer's skill. Heightened by the manner of his last two Derby victories Archer's reputation allied to his personality was now such that his appearance to ride in a race was enough to set owners of other fancied horses fearing for an unforeseen result. No one ever knew when some flash of genius would suddenly come from him to set alight the dullest race or upset a seeming certainty or carefully planned coup. 'He'd win on a donkey,' a disgusted trainer once said when Archer had dropped apparently from nowhere to get up on the post and floor a fancied runner. The fact that he was always trying made it even more difficult to assess the form of his mounts since whatever horse he was up on appeared to be transformed into running at least seven pounds better than his handicap with Archer on his back. It was all very disturbing especially when there was a great deal of money at stake.

Sir John, who was no fool beneath his bluff exterior, and who had been in racing all his life, appreciated this very well. The lurking threat of Archer on Valour to his enormous bet was in the back of his mind every day before the race. However much he reassured himself that his boastful words at Kempton were

7a. Falmouth House

7b. Fred Archer's tombstone

8. (*above*) The Duke of
Portland, about 1880

(*above, right*) Viscount
Falmouth, about 1860

(*right*) the Duke of
Westminster, about 1870

not mere talk but an accurate assessment of the form and the chances he still could not overlook Archer's apparent ability to turn sprinters into stayers and vice versa.

Lambton dined with him one night in the intervening week and he thought perhaps the old man was beginning to weaken and to change his mind about putting Archer up. He confided to Lambton that his bet was big enough to make him financially secure at least for the moment if it came off, so it must have been enormous. He went on to say that he did indeed wish that Archer could ride Peter but he felt he must remain loyal to Wood. Even so, when they went to bed that night, Lambton felt that the morning might bring about a change.

It did not. When they met Sir John told his guest in one short sentence that Wood's engagement was confirmed. He would ride Peter and that was that. Later that day Lambton met Archer and mentioned the matter to him.

'It's a pity about this,' Archer said. 'Sir John wants a turn badly and I'm afraid he won't get it now. I shall ride Valour for the Captain and he is very dangerous on that course.'

Astley and Lambton travelled to Manchester together and stayed at the Queen's Hotel, a great rendezvous for racing men at that time. Archer was there too. Such was now his fame that when he was leaving for the racecourse the next day crowds gathered outside the hotel to catch a glimpse of him. There were no pop singers in those days. Quiet-spoken, simply dressed, shy and retiring, this young man occupied in the eye of the public much the same position as the teenage idols of today. At least he repaid this adulation with exhibitions of skill, nerve, and courage.

Although Machell had determined to run Valour he had not yet shared this information with the public and rumours of all sorts were flying about concerning the race. Nat Gould, the famous writer of racing fiction, was living near Newark at the time. Tom McGeorge's hotel at Newark was, naturally enough, another rendezvous for racing men. The information to be had from the McGeorges, uncle and nephew, was usually accurate if they knew and trusted you enough to give it. Hearing stories and speculations about the race for the Cup, Gould dropped into the hotel and, chatting to young McGeorge, said that he assumed Archer would ride Peter. McGeorge corrected him, telling him that Valour ran and that Archer would ride him. Gould had backed Valour when he was beaten in the Lincoln. Wondering if there was any chance of recovering his money, he went to Manchester Racecourse and looked for Archer. Finding him, as he says, alone for once and not surrounded by admirers and hangers-on, he asked him if he fancied his chances on Valour. Archer did not say much in reply but what he did say gave Gould a strong hint that the jockey did think Valour was in with a chance. Even then, however, he could not believe that Valour would stay the distance. Nor did anyone else and Valour was freely offered at the astonishing price for one of Archer's mounts of 25–1. It was so tempting that Gould took it, but only as a saver. His real bet was on Peter.

Fully to realize what happened next it is necessary to emphasize once again that in those days races were seldom if ever ridden out from the start. Especially where a distance of ground had to be covered horses were never asked to go in the early stages. Long distance races really amounted to a strong canter followed by a sharp sprint for the post. Very often it was the point from which the sprint began that determined the race and this was dictated by the skill and timing of the rider who made his run first.

Archer knew very well that Valour had no hope of getting the trip and that if the race were truly run he was at Peter's mercy. Being Archer he had thought the thing out and decided there was a way of overcoming Valour's lack of staying power. A mile was Valour's real distance. Archer resolved to ride, as it were, two races. This is exactly what he did.

When the flag fell he set off at a good pace as if he were riding Valour over a mile. The other jockeys, afraid to make use of their horses so early, let him go. When the mile had been covered he had a commanding lead and Valour had not yet been really pushed. At the same time it was obvious that were he to continue as he was going Valour would fade out long before the finish. Using the lead he had obtained he then almost pulled Valour up, having gained the time he wanted to give him a substantial breather. He was well into the straight, hacking quietly along, before the rest came at him. Valour had now plenty of breathing space to prepare himself for the final battle. Archer set him alight. A tremendous struggle ensued between him and Peter, both horses coming right away from the field. Archer's tactics and finishing power told. He got Valour home by a neck. But he had been so saving of ground and so close to the rails that when he came in his boot was ripped open. Oblivious of the ovation which greeted him he limped to the weighing-room, changed his boots and went out for the next race.

Archer, Valour and that distance of a neck cost Sir John Astley no less than £12,000. It says much for his gameness that he accepted responsibility for his own defeat and refused to blame Wood. His disappointment was even more acute in that he had determined to buy the great Irish horse, Barcaldine, with the winnings which he had been sure would be his. He also gave Archer full credit for the victory telling someone that had it not been for Archer's jockeyship Peter could have given Valour twenty-one pounds and beaten him. This remark alone demonstrates how one very experienced owner and racing man estimated the value of Archer's services in the saddle.

Worse was to follow for Sir John. At Ascot on the day before the Hunt Cup, finding Peter was in the Queen's Vase with only 'some rips' against him, he thought he might give him a canter and make some money as well. He let him run and backed him for the certainty he looked. Again it was suggested to him that he would be wise to take Wood off and put Archer up. As obstinate as ever he scouted the suggestion, saying that this was one race Peter could not lose whoever rode him. Once more he had to pay for his opinions. At the stable turn Peter stopped dead. None of Wood's efforts could get him back into the race. Eventually he ran off the course.

Then came the Hunt Cup. This time Archer had the ride on Peter for which he had been originally engaged when Sir John had made his costly purchase. In view of the horse's defeats and misadventures Sir John looked for a good price to get back some of his losses. The public and the bookmakers, however, once Archer was up, were prepared to overlook the earlier defeats. Peter started favourite at 5–1 which was the price Sir John had to take. His losing account with the bookmakers must by now have been quite staggering.

Nor was he by this time at all as confident in his horse as he had been. He got hold of a jockey called 'Farmer' Giles who was not riding in the race, armed him with a heavy hunting whip and sent him down to the start with instructions to help Peter off by main strength if he showed any signs of reluctance to go when the flag came down. He also delivered to Archer, who hardly needed it, a homily on how to ride the horse if he began to cut it up during the race. Then, in some trepidation, he went up to the stand to watch what would happen to his money.

Peter got off all right and the hunting whip was not required. Sir John saw that with relief, but a second or so later it seemed as if his worst forebodings were about to be justified. Peter began to drop back, dig in his toes and show every sign of repeating the performance of the previous day. In fact he fell right out of the race and no one among the watching crowd believed that he would ever get into it again. But this time he had Archer on his back.

Somehow Archer kept him just on the move. Then he patted him, clucked at him and coaxed him. Gradually Peter responded to his rider. Then, suddenly, he took hold of his bit and began to race. Half a mile out he was still a long way last but clearly going so well that he was catching his field. At the distance he was with them, and at the post he had won by two lengths with 9 st. 3 lb. on his back. It was yet another astounding performance on the jockey's part. Giles, on his return, said that when he had last seen the horses he could not believe it possible for Peter to have won. In fact he thought he had no hope of even getting on terms with the other runners. If there had ever been any truth in branding Archer a mere butcher, after that race it could never be said again.

Sir John, anxious to pursue his losses now that luck had at last turned, decided to run Peter in the Hardwicke Stakes on Friday. Naturally enough he asked Archer to ride him again. Having accepted, Archer began to turn Peter's peculiarities over in his mind and to think out a way of overcoming them. Arriving at what he believed to be a solution, he went to Sir John and said: 'I have been thinking over this race, Sir John. You know the start for the mile and a half we run today is just below the spot where Peter stopped to kick on Tuesday, and it is very likely, if I canter up past it with the other horses, he may take it into his head to repeat Tuesday's performance. If you will get leave from the stewards, I will hack-canter him round the reverse way of the course and arrive at the starting post just as the other horses fall in; by so doing he may jump off and go kindly.'

This is a good example of the way in which Archer thought out his races and the problems they presented to a rider. If it were possible he left nothing to chance.

Sir John fell in with the idea and went off to see the stewards. Permission was given to him to do as Archer suggested. Timing his arrival to a nicety Archer got to the start just as they came under orders. There was no false start which was lucky, false starts being a feature of those days. Peter got away without falter or hesitation.

On this occasion Sir John had for once allowed prudence to temper his betting. He waited to see that Peter did in fact get off before he went into the ring; there, at even money, he took two bets fairish in size but by no means big for him. When Peter cantered in by eight lengths Sir John had won £1,500, but despite this and his earlier win Peter was still losing a lot of money for him. And, a little later, in the Goodwood Cup, not even Archer's cajoling could make him race. He ran out and failed to finish, thus making Astley's account even worse. All in all he was an expensive investment. Despite Peter, however, in a tally of races won in 1881 Sir John had a good year. When he came to tot up his winners, the sum being done, quite typically, on the back of one of the Rt. Hon. Jim Lowther's electioneering cards, he found that he had won 64 races, been placed second 54 times and third 31. *Ride 'em out, lad,* he wrote in his bold handwriting at the bottom of these calculations. He certainly lived up to his own advice. Like Archer he always wanted to win and it was only if he suspected that anything underhand or dishonest was going on that he became difficult and cantankerous, though he was never slow to take what he regarded as a legitimate advantage over an opponent.

As well as his adventures on Peter, Archer won the Prince of Wales Stakes at Ascot with Iroquois at the cramped odds of 5–4 on. Then he crossed to France to ride Tristan in the Grand Prix. This race, run at Longchamps on Sunday, 12th June, created an enormous amount of interest. Mr. J. R. Keene and his trainer, Sherrard, believed that they had got the American horse Foxhall, just right for it and they had engaged Fordham to ride. Many racing people in England thought Foxhall to be the best three-year-old in the country, but since he was not entered in any of the English classics this was to be the only chance he had of showing how good he was at level weights. Foxhall was, like Iroquois, American bred, being by King Alphonso out of Jamaica. He had been foaled at Woodburn, Kentucky, on 21st April 1878 and sold as a yearling to Mr. Keene for 130 sovs. But Tristan was also a useful colt. By Hermit out of Thrift his breeding was as English as the other's was American. Although owned by a Frenchman, M. Lefevre, he had done most of his previous racing in England. On the Thursday before the Grand Prix he had won a good race in supremely easy style causing his odds to be slashed from 14–1 to 7–1. It was obvious that Foxhall was going to have something to beat and the well-known rivalry between Fordham and Archer heightened the interest.

It was a glorious day and the stands were packed. Almost everyone of any consequence in English racing was there. Such was the climate of opinion of the time, however, that a considerable number of them, especially those who had any connection with Court, were nervous of being mentioned in the sporting papers as going racing on a Sunday. They requested the reporters to omit their names when writing about the scene and this request was faithfully acceded to. There was then no parade ring at Longchamps for the horses to show themselves off before the race. They were walked around as best they could be with the crowd pressing all around them and in some instances attempting to pull hairs from their tails. Tristan showed his dislike of this by lashing out and scattering the more eager. The distance was one mile and seven furlongs, the weights 8 st. 9 lb.

There was one false start and then they were away, Archer as usual being first from the flag. But on this occasion Fordham was not prepared to adopt waiting tactics or try any of his finesses. Using all the known stamina and toughness of Foxhall he headed Archer and went on to make all the running. Behind him Tristan was being nursed for his effort. Fifty yards out Foxhall looked all over a certainty, going easily in front and apparently striding away. Then Archer made his run. Two game horses and two great jockeys raced for home. They passed the post in a storm of cheering and shouting and no one in the crowd could say which had won. After a moment's wait Foxhall's number, 13, went up in the frame and the American colony went wild with delight. Foxhall, it is worth mentioning, went on to win the Cesarewitch by twelve lengths, and then to carry 9 st. in the Cambridgeshire and win, beating Bend Or, no less, at a difference of eight pounds. Tristan, useful horse though he was, was never really in that class. It again was a measure of Archer's genius and was generally accepted as such at the time, that he got him as close as he did and went so near to beating him. It was, they said, the shortest of short heads. Whatever it was it was worth £6,374 to the winner, a notable prize for those days and nearly £500 more than the value of the Derby. Archer was not best pleased at his defeat.

Back at Heath House after a comparatively lean time in the Classics recently they thought they had a champion in the making in a two-year-old filly by Skater out of Cantinière. Lord Falmouth, who always took great trouble in the naming of his horses, called her Dutch Oven. Archer won six two-year-old races with her in 1881 including the Rous Memorials at Goodwood and Newmarket and the Dewhurst Stakes. But there was nothing from Heath House for Archer in the Leger. Although Bal Gal was entered and although she had run third in the Oaks to Mr. Stirling Crawfurd's Thebais she had not really trained on. Wood was given the ride on her leaving Archer free for Iroquois.

Pincus had been preparing Iroquois for this race by his own severe methods. Sir John Astley, who watched them, said that Iroquois must have been made out of cast iron to stand up to them. Even the touts were amazed and reported on more than one occasion that he had 'gone' and could not possibly appear in the race. In the event Pincus confounded all his critics. Once more he brought out Iroquois hard and fit and muscled up. There were no signs of staleness or of his having run up light although his legs were bandaged all round and this gave rise to more rumours.

But Peregrine had been taken out and if Iroquois was sound it seemed he had no real rival. He started favourite at 2–1 and proceeded to give his backers a fright. Going over the brow of the hill he was last by some lengths and the wiseacres on the stands said that he did not look to be too happy. When they disappeared into a patch of fog which covered the course he was still last. The fog lifted and he was seen to be only just in touch with the field. Archer, however, was in his favourite place on the rails and had not moved. At the distance he came through the field and, together with Tom Cannon on Geologist, raced for home. In the end Archer won by a length, but Iroquois had scarcely been off the bit and it was then obvious that

[104]

he had only been toying with the opposition. Iroquois was a good colt in a moderate year. After this race he was taken back to America and put to stud where he was only a qualified success. Pincus stayed on, employing his own methods with a small string of horses supplied by the few owners who believed in them. He, too, had only moderate success but he became well liked and well known at Newmarket.

At that Doncaster meeting Archer won, as well as the St. Leger, the Doncaster Cup with the Duke of Beaufort's Petronel, the Portland Plate with the Duke of Portland's Mowerina, the Parkhill Plate with Bal Gal, and the Alexandra Plate with Sword Dance.

Petronel was the horse on which he had tried to get the Duke to give him the ride in the Two Thousand and on which Fordham had won that Classic. Mowerina was the first mare to be purchased by the young Duke of Portland. He bought her from Lord Rossmore for £1,200 and, like most things Portland touched when he was beginning his astounding run of luck on the Turf, she proved a wonderful bargain. The reason he bought her was because he had heard Lord Falmouth say he would like her for his own stud were she on the market. Lord Rossmore had gone down badly at the Epsom Spring Meeting and had to sell all his horses. He reckoned Mowerina to be worth £3,000 but all Portland would give him was her original price of £1,200. Rossmore had to part. 'Portland drove a very good bargain for himself,' was his comment on the transaction. She very nearly did not run in that Portland Plate at all. Weatherby, the handicapper, gave her 9 st. 5 lb., the highest weight ever given in the history of the race. Mat Dawson was not anxious to run her under that burden and told the Duke to protest. The handicapper's reply was to express courteous regret at the dissatisfaction he had caused but to recommend that they run the mare.

She did run, with Archer riding one of his cleverest and tenderest races under the big weight, and won in the end very easily. She was then a five-year-old and had one more full season's racing before her. During this she was beaten in one of the famous Archer-Fordham matches at Newmarket but she won six races for the Duke before she was retired, and £2,000 in stakes. Going to stud at Welbeck her direct produce won fifty races worth £83,000. She was the dam of Donovan who won the Derby for Portland in 1889 as well as numerous other good winners. Later on at Welbeck she was weighed against gold and it was found that she and her produce had literally won her weight in gold and 'a little over as well' as Rossmore ruefully recounted.

To crown a wonderful season Archer then won the Champion Stakes with Bend Or. The argument whether Bend Or or Robert the Devil was the better racehorse could never be resolved for they did not meet again after their match at Epsom. Bend Or did not take on Robert the Devil in the Ascot Gold Cup for it was known that he would not stay the extra distance. Robert the Devil won it much as he liked but he, in his turn, did not contest the Champion Stakes. There can, however, be no doubt at all as to which was the better sire. Bend Or transmitted his quality to his progeny and was an outstanding success at stud. Robert the Devil, a much coarser bred horse of whom Sir John Astley said that his sire, Bertram, was no more than second class and his dam, Cast-Off, not even a top-class plater, failed utterly to produce anything of note.

For Archer it had certainly been a memorable and wonderful year. He rode 220 winners including two Classics, the Derby and St. Leger. And then, after it all, he went back to Heath House and fell in love.

Chapter 7

Helen Rose Dawson was a small fair girl, gentle and pretty. She was the daughter of John Dawson, Mat's brother, who lived at Warren House, Newmarket, a few minutes' walk from Heath House. During that winter and spring Archer courted her. Both families approved of the match and soon a definite engagement was entered into. At that time the Dawsons were people of substance, and of influence in the whole racing world. When the engagement was announced a friend said to Mrs. Mathew that Helen Rose might perhaps have done better for herself than to marry a mere jockey. Though they hid their affection for him beneath a mask of gruffness no son could have been nearer to the Mathew Dawsons than Archer. Mrs. Dawson's reply was immediate and to the point. 'A princess might have aspired to marry Fred,' she said.

He had little time for hunting visits that winter and the shires saw less of him than usual. Instead he and some friends started the Newmarket Drag, and it claimed most of what free time he had. For he was very busy. Once the engagement was made formal he set about building a house worthy of his bride and her family.

Despite all the calls on his purse and his betting, which seldom went right for him, Archer was at this time a rich man. His retainers and some of the enormous fees which he could and did claim have been mentioned. With the money thus earned, save for his gambling, he was shrewd and careful. He spent all but nothing on himself, still living in the frugal quarters over the stables in Heath House; conviviality never appealed to him and, with the assistance of Lord Falmouth, his savings had been wisely and well invested. Contrary to what was said about him then and has been since, he was neither mean nor grasping but, unlike most of his fellow jockeys, he knew what money meant and he wanted it for what it could give him and the security that went with it. It was one of his tragedies that perhaps he wanted that security too much and was prepared to sacrifice too much of his health and personal life to try to get it.

Now, on some of the ground which he had bought beside the Bury Road he set about building a mansion which he had received Lord Falmouth's permission to call Falmouth House. He was later bitterly to regret the size and lavishness of the establishment he then set up, but it is at least interesting that Lord Falmouth, a shrewd and careful man about money himself, made no effort to curb his expenditure. Instead he personally supervised the plans and helped Archer in his dealings with architects and builders. This lends colour to the assumption that Archer's fortune was at that time very large. Some good judges have put it down at £250,000. It is at all events certain that Lord Falmouth would not have lent help and encouragement to the very great expenditure involved in the building of the house which was to carry his name had he not been satisfied beyond doubt that it would not in any way weaken Archer's capital position.

In fact it now appeared that Archer had all that any man would desire—fame beyond even his own wildest dreams, wealth, success, and the wife of his choice. It all seemed like a fairy-tale, someone said. But fate has a way of interfering with fairy-tales. It was in this very year, 1882, that the first of the so-called scandals affecting his name occurred and for the first time there were signs, however slight, of a rift in the great triumvirate of Falmouth, Dawson and Archer.

But, at the beginning, all went well. Winners, as usual, poured in from here, there and everywhere. Somehow, however, they were not in important races. The City and Suburban, for once, failed to come his way. Nor were there as many winners as usual from Heath House. A disagreeable thing happened, too, just after the beginning of the season which, though it had nothing to do with Archer then, was to have its repercussions upon him later on. George Alexander Baird, 'Mr. Abingdon', got himself warned off the Turf for two years.

The inner history of this warning-off has never been told and it is not within the scope of this book to try to elucidate it, but it should be mentioned that among the stewards of the Fair Oaks Easter Meeting were at least two who were known to have had a personal animus towards him. George Alexander Baird, in fact, at that time of his life, was rather too rich and did most things rather too well, including riding races and conquering women, for a parvenu, or so, had they put it in words, was the opinion of many of the ruling few. It was galling, to say the least of it, to be beaten in races and cuckolded in bed by the upstart son of a Scots ironmonger. Nor, with all his faults, which were legion, was Baird sufficiently a sycophant for his brashness and roughness to be overlooked in exchange for money and hospitality as was happening with many another aspiring merchant prince. Baird's ambitions lay on the racecourse not in the drawing-rooms of the glittering and false society of the day.

All these facts contributed to the ultimate decision to warn him off. Most of the writers of the time who have left any record of the business appear to think the sentence to have been unjust and unwarranted by the offence. What happened was that Baird won a Hunters' Selling Flat Race by eight lengths but was disqualified along with Mr. Peyton's Evenly and Lord Harrington's Gortmore for carrying the wrong weight. This would not in itself have ensured his warning-off for, if it had, Harrington would have had to go with him, but towards the end of the race he employed Archer-like tactics to get into a winning position and Archer-like language in threatening to put Harrington over the rails if he didn't give it to him. To make matters worse he is said to have greeted Harrington on their return to the weighing-room with the words: 'Sorry, my Lord. I took you for a farmer!'

Harrington, highly incensed, reported him to the Stewards of the Meeting for foul riding. He was 'sent on' to the Grand National Hunt Committee who sentenced him as has been mentioned above and this sentence was extended by the Jockey Club to all Meetings under their rules.

Since Baird's only interest and ambition in life was to ride in, and win, races—even William Allison, 'The Special Commissioner' who hated him, said that his only merit was that he rode fairly well on the flat—it may be imagined what effect the banishment had upon him. In his bitterness the rougher elements in his character, never far from the surface, began completely to dominate him. He spent much of his time in France; when he was at home he spurned the offers of sympathy from those who realized the injustice with which he had been treated. Seeking out the company of toadies, spongers, prize-fighters, and the lower strata of the *demi-monde*, he began a career of squalid dissipation which, with a brief interval, was to last until his early death eleven years later. The immense wealth had by the time he died almost all gone and one Scottish paper penned its epitaph, and Baird's, in the following words: 'All this princely fortune has been squandered on horse-racing, prize-fighting and harlotry.'

This, however, was in the future in 1882. Baird dropped out of the racing scene and few save Lambton, whose kindly nature had seen something of the good in him and realized his shyness and consciousness of establishment snubs, regretted him.

It looked like, and indeed was to prove to be, a fillies year. Mat Dawson had Dutch Oven, John Porter had two flyers in Shotover and Geheimmiss, and the Duchess of Montrose was telling everyone who would listen that her husband's Ste Marguerite would beat the lot.

Dutch Oven had not made the progress Archer and Mat Dawson had hoped for. They took her out of the One Thousand

Guineas and the Oaks, deciding to keep her for the Derby and to train her for it.

Robert Peck had retired the year before and the majority of his horses, including the Duke of Westminster's Shotover, had been sent to John Porter of Kingsclere. Porter was fortunate that year. Another rich peer, Lord Stamford, had also recently joined the stable and for him he had bought the filly Geheimmiss. Tom Cannon, who lived almost as busy a life as Archer for, besides being in the very top class of jockeys, he owned, trained and jobbed in racehorses, had bought her as a yearling for the small price of 330 guineas, solely on her looks. As a two-year-old Porter saw her and liked her and purchased her for Lord Stamford, the price being £2,000. She went through her two-year-old season unbeaten, showing blinding speed once she was asked to go. Porter decided to train her for the Oaks.

Shotover was a very different proposition. She was a delicate filly with no two-year-old form at all. But Porter, whose horses for the past few seasons had not been above handicap class, was anxious, especially with these new and prominent owners, to get back into the Classics. Realizing that the colts were not of much account he decided to go for the Two Thousand and the Derby with Shotover. Her last trial, however, proving unconvincing, they went to Newmarket with more hope than confidence. In the end she did get home, beating a bad field by a couple of lengths. Cannon rode her in this race, Archer being claimed for one of Lord Hastings'. Considering her frail constitution Porter made the extraordinary decision to run her in the One Thousand two days later. Not surprisingly she was beaten, though only by a neck and by Ste Marguerite who, like her owner's wife, was proving to be erratic in her form and temperamental in her disposition.

Porter still remained confident that in Geheimmiss he had the winner of the Oaks and he set about nursing Shotover back to her full strength and getting her ready for the Derby. Although he had changed stables the Duke of Westminster had kept his claim on Archer. Dutch Oven, too, was beginning to show them at Heath House something of her two-year-old form. It began to be obvious that if all these fillies remained sound there was going to be some conflict of interest on Archer's part sooner or later as to which he should ride. In the Derby, however, there was no question but that Lord Falmouth's first claim would be exercised and that Archer would ride Dutch Oven. Tom Cannon was re-engaged for Shotover. Riding with his usual polish he beat the 2,000 Guineas runner-up, Lord Bradford's colt Quicklime, by three parts of a length. The hot favourite, Bruce, was fourth and Dutch Oven down the field.

Doubts were cast on the merits of Shotover's victory because of the riding and running of Bruce. Mordan, his jockey, did everything wrong through the race including going wide at Tattenham Corner and dropping his hands too soon at the finish. There was talk, and for once the talk seemed well-substantiated, that certain bookmakers had been at work. Bruce was in the Grand Prix de Paris some few days later. Mordan was peremptorily taken off him and an approach was made to Archer to take the ride. A suitable fee was fixed. It has never been named but in view of the anxiety of Bruce's owners and connections to get back some of their losses and of Archer's business sense for driving a hard bargain when he could, it must have been substantial indeed. At all events he fully justified the fee for he crossed to France ten days later and won the race, giving himself revenge for last year's defeat and Bruce's stable some small consolation for a lost Derby.

Archer never cared for riding in France which was another reason why he charged huge fees for going over there. He always said that the French didn't like him, that the crowd and the jockeys were hostile to him and that both of them made it immensely difficult for him to win a race there. The crowd, he complained, bustled him and his mounts in the enclosure where there were no proper parade rings and anyone could approach the horses, and booed and hooted at him afterwards. The jockeys, too, he said, combined to try to stop him winning. In this he was most probably right. He had by now achieved such

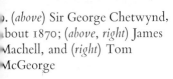

. (*above*) Sir George Chetwynd,
bout 1870; (*above, right*) James
Machell, and (*right*) Tom
McGeorge

10a. Mat Dawson, Fred Archer and St. Simon

10b. Melton: Fred Archer up. Lord and Lady Hastings

an ascendancy in England that he could get away with almost anything and frequently did. He was popular with the public and the punters because they knew they were going to get an honest run for their money when he was riding, and his fellow jockeys had come to know him and like him, apart from admiring his skill. None of these factors applied in France. He did not ride sufficiently often there for his integrity to be appreciated, and his apparent indifference to adulation or execration equally did not appeal to the Gallic temperament. The French jockeys were, naturally enough, jealous of him coming over and stealing their thunder and did what they could to prevent it. So much was this the case that on one occasion he told Lambton that he didn't care what happened or what his riding instructions were, he was going to look after himself and go round on the outside all the way.

In the meantime Porter had been becoming more and more confident that he would win the Oaks with Geheimmiss. Although he did not specifically try them against each other he was convinced that Geheimmiss was better than Shotover. He was proved right when the filly with odds of 6–4 laid on her won by two lengths from Ste Marguerite. Porter had now won two out of the first three Classics and Heath House had nothing of any account to its score.

But Archer was still riding winners. At Lewes he rode the winners of six out of the seven races. He was leading a life which demanded extraordinary resources of energy and physical stamina. Yet the steam baths and the purgations which grew more drastic every year and upon which he relied to lose weight, were putting his constitution more and more into hazard. And it was upon that constitution that his whole way of life, his success and his fortune depended. He would travel any distance to ride a fancied runner. Unlike Baird, who in his riding days would do the same, he had neither the wish nor the resources to summon up special trains to carry him all over the country. The days were long and strenuous and often ended with an exhausting hack home across the Heath from wherever the last train had dropped him. They began early, too. In his capacity as Mat Dawson's partner he now had to help supervise the stables and the working of the strings, to assist his old master with the entries and the placings of the horses, to be on hand always when he was wanted with advice or comment, or to ride out and give his opinion on the many and various horses in the yard. Devoted to him though he was, Dawson would not let him rest. The old trainer never expected to find weaknesses in his favourites whether human or equine. Indeed as he grew older he leaned on Archer more and more, relying on his flair and knowledge, the information he gleaned on his travels and his extraordinary ability to sort that information out in his mind together with his intelligence in applying it.

In addition that year Archer had to keep his eye on the builders who were constructing his mansion for him and to grapple with the many problems such an undertaking always brings with it. And there was Helen Rose with whom he was in love and whom he was going to marry. She was undemanding; she loved and admired him and gloried in his success; she had grown up with racing people, she understood his absences and the strains both mental and physical to which he was subjected. He filled her life wherever he was, but still, a lover who is seldom there and, when he is, is plagued with weight troubles, subjecting himself to steam baths and purgations and worrying about the handicapping of his horses, scarcely makes for an ideal courtship.

Besides, despite his attraction for women, he was, to use an old-fashioned expression, very much a man's man. As with many of his type his intimates, though few, were close—Machell, with whom nowadays he did much of his travelling to and from racing; McGeorge, the starter; Harry Constable, his fellow jockey with whom he once kept a train from Ascot laden with swells waiting for half an hour and whose early death left a gap in his life; and two friends of his childhood whom he never deserted, Herbert Mills, who became a prosperous corn-merchant in Cheltenham and Joseph Davis who did most of his writing and secretarial work for him. About this time, too, the strange morose, lugubrious figure of Captain Bowling came into his life. Bowling's origins appear to be in dispute. John Porter, who trained for him and to whom Archer introduced him, says he was the son of a Pembrokeshire rector; Mrs. Pratt, Archer's sister, says he belonged to the firm of solicitors Bowling and Creagh. He had served in the Zulu War and sustained a wound in his left arm, permanently crippling it and causing his retirement. A bachelor with rooms in Jermyn Street he was well-off and was able to buy and race high-class horses. There is little doubt that he sought out Archer and cultivated his friendship. Later he was almost to constitute himself the jockey's manager and someone once asked Fred if Bowling was his butler. In 1882, however, the friendship between Bowling and Archer was only just beginning. Machell, brilliant, brooding, moody and suspicious, sought for his opinions and respected his confidences; the young Lambton, at this time in the top-flight of gentlemen riders and betting his head off with the best of them, enjoyed his company, appreciated his intelligence and, as he says himself: 'admired him as a jockey and liked him as a man'. Lambton would look for him in the mornings on the Heath and elsewhere before racing, and at Goodwood he was the eyewitness of a most extraordinary mistake on Dawson's part.

Although Dawson and Archer had been disappointed with the showing of Dutch Oven in the Derby they had not given up hope of her. She seemed to be coming back to herself and they entered her in the Sussex Stakes at Goodwood and fancied her for it.

On the morning of the race Lambton hacked out with Archer to the Downs to see Dawson's horses work. Dutch Oven went a canter with the rest and, shortly afterwards, Lambton was astonished to see her doing a strong mile gallop. Archer was horrified. He went over to Dawson and reminded him that Dutch Oven was due to race that afternoon. Dawson consulted his book and realized his mistake. He had thought her race was the following Thursday.

Despite this Dutch Oven ran. Not surprisingly she was beaten into third place.

Archer, naturally enough, discounted this form, and told Lambton he thought she would win the Leger. She was then sent to York and when she won the Yorkshire Oaks easily it seemed as if Archer, as usual, was right in his judgement. Two days later, however, she was pulled out again to run in the Great Yorkshire Stakes over a distance of a mile and three-quarters and was badly beaten. There seemed to be no valid excuse save that she just did not stay. She drifted out to 40-1 in the Leger betting.

Porter had kept both Shotover and Geheimmiss for this last Classic. Dutch Oven's chances of beating them were apparently remote and Mat Dawson was despondent. He had backed Dutch Oven for the Leger after her victory in the Yorkshire Oaks. Now he commenced to lay against her. Archer, too, now reckoned her chance as hopeless. He remembered his retainer from Westminster, saw his chance of riding Shotover, and began discussions with Porter about the engagement. Porter, however, believed Geheimmiss much the better of his two fillies. Assuming that Dawson and Falmouth would not enforce their claim since Dutch Oven's chances were negligible and considering the request a mere formality, he approached the Duke of Westminster to waive his claim so that Archer could ride Geheimmiss. This the Duke most magnanimously agreed to do. Archer's riding fee had then to be fixed with Lord Stamford. He asked for £1,000 and got it.

At no time had these negotiations been disclosed to either Dawson or Falmouth. It was only after the fee was agreed that Archer, his hopes of riding another classic winner now high, approached Dawson for the expected permission. To his consternation he was met with a blank refusal. Dawson, even then, knew nothing about Westminster's abandonment of the second claim and the arrangements for riding Geheimmiss. He assumed that Archer would ride the Duke's filly. 'You may as well get beaten on Dutch Oven as on Shotover,' he told him.

Archer was furious. He had lost his chance of riding the favourite, Geheimmiss, which he now thought to be a certainty, he had lost his special fee, and all, he told a friend, to have to ride a filly which had not one chance in a thousand. There was, for the first time, something approaching a coolness between the Heath House partners. Porter, too, was put out since he could not now get Tom Cannon for the favourite.

The feeling between the Heath House partners was not improved by the decision to run Lord Falmouth's good two-year-old Gaillard in the Champagne Stakes. Gaillard had won his two previous races but in the second, the Prince of Wales's Stakes at York, he had run while coughing and he had not recovered from this by the time Doncaster came round. Nevertheless he ran, was well backed by the stable, ridden by Archer and finished last. This was the day before the St. Leger, the Tuesday, and no one connected with Gaillard, including the owner, was best pleased with the result.

On the morning of the race Geheimmiss, to be ridden by Loates, was 13-8 on. Dutch Oven was still at 40-1 offered and with very few takers. Archer's money, one can be sure, was on the favourite.

When the field got away Dutch Oven looked like bearing out everyone's gloomy predictions. She was last half a mile from home and appeared sure to stay there. Then Archer got at her. To the astonishment of everyone, including her rider, she began to run through the field. What was more, it was seen that the two Kingsclere cracks were in trouble. Archer then began to ride for all he was worth. Dutch Oven caught and passed Shotover and collared Geheimmiss. The favourite was beaten in a few strides. Dutch Oven coasted on to win by a length and a half. The victory was greeted in stony silence. Her recent running was uppermost in everyone's minds. There had already been the scandal over the Derby and the air that year was thick with suspicion.

Sir John Astley who, as has been said, could be an interfering busybody at times, was the first to give voice to the general suspicion. He did it, as was his wont, promptly and with emphasis. Coming down from the stand he went straight to the stewards and prevailed upon them there and then to hold an inquiry into the form of the runners and the riding of the race.

John Corlett, the owner and editor of the *Pink 'Un*, who regarded many of Sir John's activities with an amused scepticism, had a pretty good idea of what would happen to his objection and he kept a note of the immediate sequence of events. Here is what he wrote down:

At 3 h 18m 16s Dutch Oven won the St. Leger.

At 3h 18m 40s Sir John Astley requested that Lord Falmouth, Mathew Dawson, and Frederick James Archer be summoned to appear before the Stewards of the meeting to enquire into the running of Dutch Oven in the Great Yorkshire Stakes.

At 3h 19m 2s the Honble H. W. Fitzwilliam, M.P., the Earl of Durham, and the Duke of Beaufort, the Stewards of the meeting, were of the opinion that no sufficient case had been made out for any action on their part.

But if the Stewards cleared Archer the public did not. The punters and the gutter Press were free in their accusations. Wherever racing was discussed, in bars and clubs where the would-be knowing foregathered, it was stated over and over again that Archer had pulled Dutch Oven at Goodwood and York in order to get a long price for himself. In fact nothing could have been farther from the truth. If Archer's money had been on her, Dutch Oven would have started at a price far shorter than 40-1. Archer had done everything he could to avoid riding her and had been annoyed at losing his special and splendiferous fee from Lord Stamford. In addition, if he backed Geheimmiss and it is all but certain that he did, he had lost that money as well.

To cap it all he had to give Kitty, the racecard seller, a new bonnet. When she had wished him luck in the Leger he had laughed and said that if he won she should have a new bonnet from him to replace the one she was wearing. He forgot all about this promise until she waylaid him in Newmarket High Street on the morning of the Cesarewitch and loudly called for payment. He had very little money with him—this was another of his peculiarities—and Kitty would not let him go until he had paid up. Fumbling in his pockets for money which was not there, he was receiving all the time a berating from Kitty's tongue for his meanness and Kitty's tongue was well used to holding her own in rougher company than his. A crowd was beginning to gather when a friendly newspaper-man came along, inquired what was happening, and redeemed his pledge for him.

The rumblings and recriminations went on as the season drew to a rather dreary end. It was the first time he had been openly and widely accused of chicanery and he hated it. He knew the accusations to be untrue which made them all the harder to bear. The explanation of Dutch Oven's performance which he and Mat Dawson had arrived at was that they had run her too soon and in ground too heavy for her in the Great Yorkshire Stakes and that she had only really come to herself by St. Leger day. John Porter said afterwards that neither of his two fillies had any pretensions to staying the Leger distance anyway, an explanation which might have been more convincing had he offered it before the race and not made such efforts to get Archer to ride Geheimmiss. Lambton said that he didn't think any of them was a true stayer and this may have been the real explanation of the whole affair since the colts that year were a useless lot and the three fillies occupied the first three places in the St. Leger the first and only time this has ever happened. Archer and Dawson seemed to be vindicated when Dutch Oven with a shade of odds laid on her won both the Great Foal Stakes and the Triennial Produce Stakes at Newmarket. But the rumblings and whisperings and knowing smiles persisted just the same, with results which were to blossom out into the full flower of rumour and scandal the following year.

Chapter 8

It is hardly necessary to say that he was champion once again in 1882, this time with 210 winners. After the season ended he went back to Newmarket to see about getting Falmouth House finished and to prepare for his marriage. This took place at the Church of All Saints, Newmarket, on 31st January 1883. Presents from the great and the humble alike had poured in for weeks before. Lord Falmouth sent a silver dinner service which, with typical thoughtfulness, he had not had engraved lest others had sent the same thing.

Prince Batthyany gave the bride a jewelled bracelet 'set with a pearl as large as a brazil nut, round which were girdles of diamonds', to wear on her wedding day. The groom's present to the bride was a lucky diamond horseshoe. There were those who said that the couple did not need luck. They were to prove false prophets.

Helen Rose, who was given away by her father John Dawson, wore a satin dress trimmed with silk lace and the four bridesmaids coral silk gowns and diamond and pearl bracelets given them by the groom. The church seats were filled, not with the nobility and gentry, the rich and the great, but with relatives and close friends of the bride and groom. John Porter was there and Robert Peck, McGeorge the starter, Joe Davis and Herbert Mills, all the Dawson family and, needless to say, bursting with pride, Archer's father and mother.

Special trains were run from outlying villages to bring ad-

mirers to the scene. Newmarket was packed with excited throngs
who cheered the bride and groom all the way to the station
where a special carriage awaited them on a siding. Their progress to London almost amounted to that of a royal couple.
Cambridge station was packed with people to cheer them as they
passed.

When they had gone John Dawson entertained the guests to a
ball at the Rutland Arms; the stable lads were given a lavish
supper in the Wagon and Horses; an ox, presented by Lord
Hastings, was roasted whole on the Severals and consumed by
the assembled company. An exciting and hectic day ended with
the flying of balloons and a firework display.

The honeymoon was spent at Torquay and, even there,
'the swells' pressed their attentions on the couple. The Duchess
of Sutherland came to call but found them out; and Lord
Courtenay issued invitations—which were not accepted—for a
visit to Powderham Castle.

Archer did not stay long away from the hub and meaning of
his life—Newmarket and racehorses. Soon he was back at Falmouth House and he and his bride were settling in. Large though
the place was with its long dining-room, spacious drawing-
room, breakfast-room, conservatory, even a private, two-
roomed Turkish bath for Archer's own use, it was packed with
valuables. There were gold and silver racing cups in profusion,
spoils of a great career hitherto locked away in a bank; portraits
by the leading artists of the day of Archer on his Classic winners
and other great or favourite horses, a signed picture of the Prince
of Wales and many of the valuable wedding presents presented
by 'the swells' and others. Amongst these was a knick-knack he
particularly valued, a silver cigarette box from Lord Charles
Beresford mounted on a portion of a shell which had burst on
the *Condor* at the bombardment of Alexandria. There were,
too, photographs of his old friends Harry Constable and Tom
McGeorge, and engravings of the Duke of Westminster and Lord
Falmouth. His shotgun was by Purdy and in the cellars were
about two hundred dozen of champagne and other wines.

During the honeymoon there had been a series of burglaries at Newmarket. Hearing of these, on his return, Archer became worried for his treasures. He searched for and found a revolver which had been given him by Mr. Thomas Roughton when his horse, Sterling, won the Liverpool Cup. Loading it he placed it in a drawer of the pedestal table beside his bed. It was to remain there unused for only a little over three years.

When he came back there was, too, the news of the death in Cannes of an old friend and supporter, the Duchess of Montrose's second husband W. S. Stirling Crawfurd. Crawfurd had been a lavish spender on the Turf, and had not, on the whole, received a great deal in return by way of success financial or otherwise. But his fortune was vast and nothing in the way of reverses appeared to upset him in the least or to modify his expenditure. Until his marriage at the age of fifty-seven to the Duchess of Montrose he had been one of the most popular and respected figures on the Turf. Thenceforward that formidable woman had largely dictated the management of his racing interests. Touchy, vindictive, savagely outspoken, rich, raddled and ruthless, Caroline Duchess of Montrose was known to her intimates as Carrie or sometimes as Carrie Red from the one-time colour of her hair, and to the younger set as Six Mile Bottom. She was sixty-seven years of age when she married Mr. Crawfurd, masterful, domineering and set in her ways which were eccentric in the extreme. She changed her trainers almost as often as she changed her mind which was every other day and sometimes every other hour; about the only person who could deal with her was Alec Taylor of Manton, 'Grim old Alec', who stood no nonsense and went his own way, forestalling her instructions, circumventing the most wayward of her directions and—producing winners for her. She waged a constant verbal battle with Captain Machell when they were neighbours at Newmarket; should anyone cross her she did not hesitate to say what she thought of him in the most vivid terms in any company and to all who would listen. Many of her remarks are too well-known to repeat but her encounter with the portly Major

Egerton, the handicapper, illustrates the sharpness of her tongue and the pungency of her conversation. She thought, almost certainly without reason, that Egerton was unfair in his handicapping of her horses. In the Birdcage at Newmarket and in the hearing of all she said to him at the top of a very carrying voice: 'I presume, Major Egerton, from the way you handicap my horses, you are anxious to ride them yourself. I can only say that your ambition will not be gratified.' 'Ah, Mr. Peace—the Peace that passeth all understanding,' she greeted one of her trainers when she was about to dismiss him. And she roundly trounced her vicar, whose living was in her hands, for praying for fine weather when he very well knew, so she said, that she was running a horse next day that needed the going deep.

But it cannot have been pleasant for Mr. Crawfurd to have his colours publicly hissed at Newmarket only a few months before he died because the Duchess insisted on an eleventh-hour scratching of the well-fancied Thebais. Worse still, though he had not wanted to be present, she subjected him to the public ignominy of appearing and then being well-nigh driven to leave the course by the cat-calls and jeering of an angry crowd.

Mr. Crawfurd's colt, Macheath, the last good animal he ever owned, had won the Middle Park Plate in 1882 defeating Archer on Highland Chief, who was trained by his brother Charles Archer. Macheath went on to win the Criterion and would have retired unbeaten had not the Duchess insisted on his being pulled out again on the following Friday when he was trounced by the only horse left in to oppose him. Macheath was well-fancied to win the Guineas the following year but by the prevailing rule on his owner's death all his nominations became void. Even then this rule was much criticized but it took forty-five years and a law case to change it.

Besides Macheath Mr. Crawfurd had other good horses in training at his death including Thebais, Ste Marguerite and Corrie Roy. He had also just purchased Isonomy as a stallion for 9,000 guineas. There was considerable speculation as to what would happen to these horses but it was soon resolved for the Duchess announced that she would continue to control and race them, but that out of respect, she would lease the horses for one year to Sir Frederick Johnstone in whose name they would run for that year.

Almost immediately she came searching for Archer's services as a jockey. She had a weakness for handsome young men. Devoid of scruple, she had had her eye on Archer for some time and was probably half in love with him even then. The fortune left her by her husband had been immense. She offered Archer £6,000 for a claim of any sort. Never averse to a bargain, Archer demurred. It is said that she then proffered him a blank cheque. She got her claim. The final figure has never been divulged but, if one considers the resources at her command and her wish to have her own way and sets these against Archer's shrewdness where sums of money were in question one is safe in assuming it was truly enormous.

Archer had, then, even more claims on his purse than was usual. He had to finish with the builders and decorators, arrange for the running of a large establishment, very different from his two frugal rooms, and to provide for his wife and a future family. But for the first and perhaps the only time in his life he appeared wholly relaxed and happy. Some time later he was to tell a friend that he believed he had fulfilled all his dreams. He was the reigning champion in his chosen sphere of life, he had married the girl he loved, he thought nothing could go wrong for him ever again. It is a dangerous state of mind to be in.

At first, however, all looked set fair for another wonderful year. He won the Two Thousand Guineas on Gaillard beating Tom Cannon on Goldfield by a head after a terrific finish. When he came in he heard the news that Prince Batthyany had dropped dead almost at the feet of Lord Charles Beresford and the Duke of Portland as they were entering the Jockey Club rooms. Gaillard was by Galopin who had won the Derby for the prince some years before and it was thought that the excitement of the race had over-taxed the old man's weak heart. Shortly afterwards it was announced that the prince's horses, then trained by

John Dawson, would be put up for auction after the July New-market Meeting.

Lord Falmouth, who was now getting old and whose health was troubling him, was most anxious to add another Derby to his successes, for he was already talking in private about his re-tirement from the Turf. After the Guineas result he thought that with Gaillard he must have every chance of doing it.

But, despite the fact that Macheath had lost his chance owing to the death of his owner, there were two other very live Derby contenders. The first of these was Highland Chief, the colt that Macheath had only just beaten in the Middle Park Plate. Archer had ridden him then and, since he rode work for his brother whenever he could, he rode him now at home in his Derby preparation. Highland Chief was a leggy colt and Archer told his brother that he did not much fancy his chances at Epsom. Although Archer did not know it Sir George Chetwynd who, to use his own words, was then backing Gaillard with 'more money than I have ever had on a horse in the Derby before', was at the same time having his own reservations about the Heath House colt owing to his heaviness of shoulder.

The finish of the Two Thousand had been a hectic one with no less than five horses in the final shake up. Highland Chief had been the fifth of these and had been running on so that Charles Archer had some justification for his Derby hopes. The colt immediately in front of Highland Chief had been St. Blaise. Trained by John Porter for Lord Alington and Sir Frederick Johnstone, two most experienced racing men, at first no one realized how good St. Blaise was. He was by Hermit who had also been the sire of Shotover and, like Shotover, he had done nothing of much account during his two-year-old career. As a three-year-old he was stopped in his early work owing to the flooding of the gallops at Kingsclere. He became gross in condi-tion and Porter really only ran him in the Two Thousand in order to put a race into him. The trainer was pleasantly sur-prised at his colt's forward showing and after that race started him in strong work for the Derby. St. Blaise improved as each day passed and Porter and the owners began to have very real hopes of success at Epsom.

A week before the Derby Porter staged one of his famous trials and the Prince of Wales being a close personal friend of Alington's was invited down to see it. Geheimmiss and Shotover, now four-year-olds, Incendiary, a good six-year-old handicapper, together with St. Blaise were to be sent over the full Derby distance. Geheimmiss was set to give St. Blaise 13 lb., Shotover 6 lb. and Incendiary to receive 4 lb. St. Blaise won by two lengths from Incendiary and Shotover. The trial, Porter commented, was, in fact, a truly run race. He decided that at worst it was going to take something very good to beat his colt.

News of the trial leaked out and St. Blaise's price shortened. Despite this and the presence of Gaillard in the field, Charles Archer refused to have his confidence in Highland Chief shaken. Like his brother when he gambled he went for high stakes. He was determined to back Highland Chief and back him he did to the tune of standing to lose £1,000 if the colt was beaten and to collect something astronomical if he won.

Webb was engaged for Highland Chief, Wood was on St. Blaise and Archer, of course, rode Gaillard who started favourite at 100–30.

Galopin colts were as a rule highly-strung and temperamental and Gaillard was no exception. When he was exercised on the course the day before the Derby it was noticed that he had pulled up in a lather of sweat. On the morning of the race he was nervous and fractious in the box. Dawson secured permission from the stewards to take him out of the preliminaries and the parade. Mounted on his cob the trainer preceded Gaillard to the course where Archer met them. They went through the milling crowd on the hill to the start where Gaillard was saddled. So those in the enclosure that year had no sight of the favourite at all.

The race had attracted enormous interest and it was one of the biggest crowds for years. Lord Rosebery had issued no less than 1,200 tickets to enable the fortunate bearers of them to approach

[126]

and leave the course through the gardens at the Durdans, his Epsom seat. He was there, of course, along with the swells and the knowing, the clever and the needy of the racing world and the vast mass of punters who had gathered for the show. The names of the three horses—Gaillard, Highland Chief and St. Blaise—were on everybody's lips. Already rumours were going through the crowd like wildfire that something shady was afoot concerning the running of the race.

At least Gaillard caused no trouble at the start. McGeorge got them all away together at the first attempt without any false starts.

No one will ever know what really happened in that race and in itself it constitutes the greatest question mark of Archer's career. Did he or did he not stop Gaillard in an effort to let up Highland Chief and save his brother's money?

It is certain that Wood on St. Blaise got Archer's usual berth —the inside—at Tattenham Corner. Fordham, riding in his last Derby and on a course he never liked, went wide and took some of the others with him. Immediately Wood opened up a lead from the rest of the field. Gaillard and Goldfield went after him and Highland Chief, hard ridden, began to close on these two. Goldfield dropped back beaten but Highland Chief caught Gaillard and they ran on together under pressure. Then Highland Chief appeared to master Gaillard and to creep up level with St. Blaise. A battle for the post ensued and the two of them went past it together with Gaillard just behind.

'By God we're done!' Sir Frederick Johnstone said to Lord Alington as he put down his glasses. But the judge gave it to St. Blaise by a neck and placed Gaillard third, half a length behind.

Hardly had the horses been led in than talk and rumours began to fly about. It was common property that Charles and Fred Archer were close friends besides being brothers, and Charles, in his usual way, had not been reticent about the amount of money with which he had backed his horse. The Dutch Oven affair of the previous season was dragged up again. Many good judges, and those who considered themselves to be good judges, on the stands, were of the opinion that Archer had not thrown himself into the finish as he had done on Bend Or and Iroquois and, had he done so, that he must have won. It was also said that Highland Chief, with Gaillard out of the way, would have won if Webb had timed his run better, and indeed Webb afterwards admitted to having ridden a bad race. So that if Archer, for the first time in his life, did less than his best in a Classic race, he did it to no avail.

Soon open accusations of his having thrown the race were made both verbally and in the Press. His enemies—and his aloofness and self-containment had made him enemies—in addition to the jackals who are always ready to snarl at success, howled at him and denigrated him. The sensational Press printed lurid stories. Fuel unfortunately was added to the fire when Lord Falmouth chose that moment publicly to announce his withdrawal from racing and to say that his entire stud of stallions, brood mares and horses in training would be offered for sale the following spring.

It has been claimed that Lord Falmouth's decision had nothing to do with the running of that Derby but the coincidence of his announcement makes this unlikely. Even the best and most tolerant of owners has his off days, his moments of doubt and suspicion, times when his ears are open when they should be shut to the voices of rumour, spite and scandal. There had been, too, the business of Archer trying to get off Dutch Oven and the running of Gaillard, when he was obviously wrong the year before and yet had been heavily backed, to raise seeds of doubt in his mind. His health, too, was far from good and may have made him more receptive than he might have been to misinterpreting motives and entertaining rumour. Also he had been privately considering retiring for some little time. But there can be little doubt that Gaillard's Derby was the culminating factor in his final decision, although later on he himself seems to have realized that it may well have been too hastily made. The great triumvirate that had reigned so proudly and so long and had collected no less than thirteen classic races in eight years was split asunder.

Being the man he was, a worrier, a solitary, reserved, introspective and proud of his good name, the accusations hurt Archer terribly, especially after the high hopes with which he had begun the season, the first of his married life. He was not much company for his young wife those days, he was driven in on to himself and only to his closest intimates would he admit how much he resented the scandal and the actions of those who believed it.

Did he in fact do less than his best on Gaillard? Lambton unhesitatingly backed him up and would hear no word against him. But Lambton was a champion; his friends could do no wrong, his enemies no right; and Archer was a close friend, a man for whom the young Lambton had both respect and admiration. Sir George Chetwynd declared that Gaillard lost because his heaviness in the shoulder prevented him coming down the hill. Few people knew more of racing than Sir George and he was, besides, talking against his own money. But the race was not lost on the hill or round Tattenham Corner. It was lost at the finish. Wood was Sir George's man and he was always anxious, then and thereafter, to try to see that no suspicion of unfairness should attach to any race in which Wood rode, especially if he won. Sydenham Dixon and William Allison, both responsible journalists, and perhaps the leading Turf writers of the day, far removed from the gutter Press which made its living by slinging accusations about, both had their doubts concerning the truth of the running and expressed them.

Nevertheless, when all is said and done it seems most unlikely that Archer did anything to interfere with Gaillard's chances. If he did he acted wildly out of character. His one ambition was to win races, especially Classic races. In these he could almost be described as the will to win incarnate as his previous victories had shown. He had just been married and had won one Classic —what more natural than for him to wish to crown his first year of married life with another Derby victory? As for betting he had been known before to ride some of his best races when his money was elsewhere than on the horse he was riding so that in the event of his having backed Highland Chief, a horse he disliked and whose chances he discounted, that fact was not likely to deter him. Nor was his friendship and affection for his brother a conceivable influence on his riding of the race. Friendship and affection counted for nothing with Archer once he was on a racehorse. In his riding days he had, as we know, once put his brother over the rails when he tried to steal the inside from him. It is quite beyond belief that he would have stopped a colt belonging to his best owner to help his brother out. Moreover the effects of his bet and of the loss of his race on Charles Archer have been exaggerated. Charles was of much tougher fibre mentally than Fred and unlikely to be knocked out by one blow, however severe. He would get the money together from somewhere for another gamble and come again. In fact that was what he did. The following day he had a horse called Lowland Chief running. With Webb up once more Lowland Chief, carrying every penny Charles Archer could lay hands upon, got up in the last stride to beat a roaring favourite trained by Captain Machell. All Charles' losses on the Derby were made good by that victory and he even came out something on the right side as a result of it.

Although they persisted to the end of his days and long after it all the evidence seems to show that so far as Archer was concerned those rumours of his fixing that Derby were unfounded. Even Lord Falmouth appears, at least tacitly, afterwards to have admitted this for he kept on a few horses in training when his sale was over and Archer rode them for him.

But just the same, fate seemed to be turning against him. Porter sent St. Blaise to Longchamps for the Grand Prix de Paris, and engaged Archer to ride him. The French jockeys made a dead set at him. Not all his strength and cursing and cleverness could get him through in time. Although he did free himself from the scrimmage in the end it was just too late and he was beaten by what Porter called 'half a neck'.

Then Gaillard, ridden by Archer, went on to win the Prince of Wales's Stakes at Ascot from Ossian and on the following day Ossian beat Archer on St. Blaise for second place in the Ascot Derby. Gaillard won the St. James's Palace Stakes on Thursday and the Triennial Stakes on Friday each time ridden by Archer and each time winning with something in hand.

The excuse made for St. Blaise, and there is little doubt but that it was a valid one, was that he was run too soon after his hard race in France but the public did not so accept it and these results renewed the discussion and controversy over the Derby, and brought a fresh flood of recrimination down on Archer's head. He was back in France again, however, to ride Frontin, who had beaten St. Blaise at Longchamps, in the Prix du Jockey Club. This time he made sure he did not get into trouble and came home a winner at 5–4. St. Blaise, as it so happened, was never of much account afterwards and when he began to suffer from leg trouble he was sold to America as a stallion. There he was passed on for £20,000 to a professional gambler called Charles Read. Soon after the sale he was burnt to death in a fire at Read's stables. There was no insurance cover and Read lost the whole of his purchase price.

During July Prince Batthyany's horses came up for sale at Newmarket. At this time the Duke of Portland, still a comparative tyro on the Turf, was looking for something to carry his colours into prominence. He had his eye on Fulmen, one of the horses in the sale, and he took Mat Dawson along to look at him.

In the next box to Fulmen was a two-year-old called St. Simon. They both liked the colt but noticed that one of his hocks had been given a dressing which looked like a blister. Dawson ran his hand over it, said that there was no curb and that he thought the dressing smelt more like paint than a blister. He also muttered something about 'me brother John', and told Portland that he would have a word or two to say to his brother when next they met. On the way home they discussed the horses they had seen and Dawson advised Portland that if he didn't get Fulmen he should certainly try for the other. They neither of them had the faintest idea of what they were about to buy.

Unknown to Dawson and Portland the news had been sent to Sir George Chetwynd, who missed very little of what was going on, that St. Simon was a 'flyer', that he had his leg dressed to look like a blister, but that he should take no notice of it and be sure to buy the colt. Sir George, as usual, was finding ready cash not too plentiful, but he had a commission to buy a horse for a price around a thousand pounds. He had not time before the auction to get firm instructions as to what price he should go to, nor could he find out anything further about the blistered leg.

Dawson failed to get Fulmen for the Duke, being outbid by 500 guineas. He had been unable to see his brother John in the meantime but he determined nevertheless to secure St. Simon. The colt was knocked down to him at 1,600 guineas, Portland's instructions to Dawson in the bidding being to go on until he was told to stop. As it turned out this was probably the greatest bargain ever to be made in the sale ring. Sir George Chetwynd who still had some reservations about the leg, and in any event did not know the exact limit of his customer's price, was the runner-up.

After the sale Dawson and Portland went to John to ask about the colt. John confined himself to saying he thought the colt just about worth the money and that he could go a bit. But John Dawson had in fact tried St. Simon that January with a good handicapper of his called Dart. Fred Smith, one of his stable lads, saw the trial and said afterwards that his master knew very well what St. Simon could do. Almost certainly it was the result of this trial which was conveyed to Chetwynd, and it would also explain 'the blister' and why Dawson could not find his brother before the sale. There can be little doubt that John Dawson was hoping to secure the colt for himself or one of his patrons.

Dawson brought the colt home and next morning the Duke came down to see him work. He was profoundly disappointed.

He disliked St. Simon's action and way of going and told Dawson that the colt could not 'stride over a straw'. The Duke of Portland was never at any time a great judge of a horse or rider but he had beneath his fashionably vapid and foppish exterior a certain instinctive shrewdness where money was concerned. This was immediately evident from what happened next in the story of St. Simon. Robert Peck, who also knew a thing or two, hearing that Portland was unimpressed with his purchase, sent him a message saying he would take St. Simon and give the Duke a profit of 400 guineas. Portland immediately sensed that there were those about who knew more of the colt's promise than he did and that if he was worth that to Peck he was worth keeping to him. He thanked Peck for his offer and told Dawson he would hold on to St. Simon.

All Prince Batthyany's nominations had, of course, become void owing to his death but St. Simon had not in any case been entered for the Derby owing, Portland thought, to the Prince's dislike of the Epsom course.

Dawson and Portland set about making new engagements and decided to start the colt's career at Goodwood.

St. Simon was by Galopin and, like Gaillard and indeed most of Galopin's descendants, he had inherited much of his sire's highly-strung temperament. He was a bay or brown horse, well put together and slightly on the leg. At Heath House, before he was in strong work, he was quiet enough in his box. Once he started to become fit his temperament manifested itself and made him exceedingly difficult to do. It was necessary to put a muzzle on him before attempting to groom him and, even then, one man had to be stationed at his head while another strapped him. In time he became fairly tractable in the hands of one man and one man only, C. Fordham, the lad who was placed in charge of him from the first. If anyone else came near him he would chase him out of the box. Always a profuse sweater, sometimes in summer his rug would never be really dry. He was a horse that required constant attention and no one save Fordham was capable of giving it to him; lads handed in their notice to Dawson rather than face the task of being set to groom the colt. Even boxing him to go by rail to a race-meeting was difficult and sometimes took hours. Finally Fordham found that he went in with least trouble if he were backed up to the box and that was the method they adopted. When Sydenham Dixon said to Fordham that St. Simon took patience to look after he received the answer: 'Patience! Talk about Job, sir, Job's never done a St. Simon!' Later on, when he was at stud at Welbeck, the Duke of Portland found that the only thing he was afraid of was an umbrella!

Before Goodwood they tried him with a useful filly, Clochette, setting St. Simon to give her a stone. The result of this trial whatever it was, for Portland and Sydenham Dixon have left differing accounts of it, pleased the stable. Ridden by Archer, St. Simon was expected to and did win the two races at Goodwood for which he was entered without being in the least troubled. His next race was the Devonshire Nursery at Derby and here he really began to show the measure of his greatness. He did not start favourite. That honour was given to Robert Peck's colt Archer, named after the jockey, to whom St. Simon was set to give 17 lb. He carried 8 st. 12 lb. and had to give away weights ranging from 9 to 40 lb. This he did with contemptuous ease. Ridden by Archer he won by two lengths without ever being off the bit or asked a question. He was then sent to Doncaster to run in the Prince of Wales's Nursery over seven furlongs. Here he had 9 st. to carry and was giving 3 st. 2 lb. to the bottom weight and 1 st. 3 lb. to the nearest in the handicap to him. The field to which he had to give this astonishing range of weights was a useful one and he slammed it. Archer never cared about unduly exposing a promising two-year-old but St. Simon's immense strength and stride surprised and overpowered even him. He won by eight lengths with the field spreadeagled behind him. Amongst them was St. Medard who was to come into Archer's life the following year.

After this race Mat Dawson wrote to a friend: *I hope you will come to the Houghton Meeting to see St. Simon. He is certainly the best two-year-old I have ever trained—he will probably make the best racehorse who ever ran on the Turf.*

The reason behind this letter was that John Porter had in his stable a very good colt belonging to the Duke of Westminster called the Duke of Richmond. Before Goodwood he had come through one of Porter's searching trials with flying colours and he had won the Richmond Stakes there easily. The Duke of Portland who, as has been said, was not a very good judge of horses, remarked to Dawson that Westminster's colt was a very nice one and he hoped that one day he could own his equal. Dawson told him that he thought he did indeed own one now just as good, if not better, in St. Simon. Their engagements did not clash and since they were both obviously the best of their year a match was arranged between them. This was to be for 500 guineas a side and was to take place over the Bretby Stakes course after the Newmarket Houghton Meeting.

Tom Cannon was engaged to ride Duke of Richmond. As the horses were being led around before going out for this match Portland in some manner contrived to hear Porter's riding instructions to his jockey. 'Jump off, Tom, and cut the beggar's throat from the start,' Porter said. Portland conveyed what he had heard to Dawson who immediately turned to Archer. 'You will be good enough to do the same,' he told him, 'and I have no doubt, mon, that you will do it with success.'

Archer obeyed his instructions exactly. He was twenty lengths ahead by the time quarter of a mile had been covered. Then he gave St. Simon a breather and allowed Cannon to get to his girths. The two jockeys put on a show for the watchers but St. Simon won with an immense amount in hand by three parts of a length. 'That's the best two-year-old I have ever seen in my life,' was Mat Dawson's only remark after the race. St. Simon was then put by for the following year.

Lord Falmouth, too, had a pair of useful two-year-olds in the colt Harvester and the filly Busybody. Archer won the Clearwell Stakes on Harvester and the Middle Park on Busybody, the first time, incidentally, that Lord Falmouth had won this important race. Archer ended the season heading the list once again with 232 wins, his best aggregate to date, and a record, but no one could pretend it had been a happy year. There had been, too, amongst all the other rows and scandals and disagreements another humiliating defeat in a match at Newmarket by Fordham.

Leopold de Rothschild had engaged Archer to ride Brag for £200 a side in a match against Reputation. Brag was set to give Reputation a stone and Fordham was to ride Reputation.

Archer had already been beaten several times by Fordham that Newmarket week. He was determined that, on this occasion, he would have his revenge.

'Mind the old man don't do you again,' someone called to him as he was going out of the gate.

'I will be half-way home this time before the old gentleman knows where he is,' Archer called back.

Unfortunately for Archer, Custance, who was perhaps Fordham's closest friend and who had been best man at his wedding, heard the exchange and repeated it to Fordham. 'All right, Cus,' was all that Fordham said. But he laid himself out to exert every inch of his skill to make a fool of Archer. What is more, he succeeded.

Brag, at the weights, needed to be held up for one run, for which he had a considerable turn of speed. But Fordham 'kidded' Archer into believing he had stolen a start and could make the best of his way home. Then it was he who came with one beautifully timed run and beat Archer by a neck. 'Archer,' Custance said, 'was persuaded by Fordham into making too much use of his horse at the worst of the weights.' This was the occasion that Archer flung the saddle across the changing-room, swearing and saying: 'I can't beat that kidding bastard.'

There were signs, also, that all was not as well as it might be between Portland and Archer. Lord Falmouth's coming retirement, too, and the thought of the dispersal of that magnificent string, for he had not altered his impulsive decision, cast a gloom over the stable. These were things which affected

Archer's professional life. His personal life, in addition, was causing him worry.

Helen Rose, who was with child, was far from well; Charles Archer, his brother, had his permit to train on Newmarket Heath withdrawn by the Jockey Club; and the demands on his purse by his parents were steadily increasing.

Chapter 9

In January 1884 a son was born to Frederick and Helen Rose Archer. It scarcely survived birth and died in a few hours. Helen Rose was desperately ill and remained so for weeks. Archer, helping with getting the Heath House horses ready, trying to look after his many and varied racing interests, was distracted with grief and worry. He galloped his hack Scotch Pearl to and from Cambridge to Falmouth House, covering the distance in times which astounded those who heard of them. Every minute he could spare was spent at his wife's bedside. Gradually, slowly, she grew better.

It was a hard winter and they were worried, too, about St. Simon. Always fractious, with his exercise cut down to being led around on a straw track, he became virtually unmanageable. He kicked and fought and continually got off the track on to the ice. No less than seventeen times (Fordham counted them) in the course of one week he slipped up and they could scarcely believe it when he was seen to have suffered no injury. But when the thaw came and he was brought out on to the Heath to work he appeared quite unlike his former self, being lazy and unwilling to gallop. All his old fire seemed to have gone. Dawson told Archer to ride him a strong gallop and wake him up.

Fordham, who knew St. Simon better than anyone else, distrusted this apparent placidity. When he put Archer up he saw he was wearing spurs and suggested that he should take them off. Archer did not take kindly to advice, especially when he was worried or upset. Fordham was pretty smartly put in his place.

Everything seemed normal about the gallop until Archer touched the colt with the spur. Then St. Simon came to life with a vengeance. He simply took away with the jockey and nothing even Archer could do would stop him. They burst through another trainer's string and disappeared. Dawson and Portland, who were on their hacks, went after the pair, dreading what they would find. They came up with Archer near the town where the Limekilns ended. He was off the horse and had the reins over his arm. On Dawson angrily asking him what he had thought he was doing he answered: 'So long as I live I will never touch that animal again with a spur; he's not a horse, he's a blooming steam engine.'

As a matter of fact he never got another chance for he never rode St. Simon, at least in a race, again. No one knows what happened between him, Portland and Dawson. Whether Portland was dissatisfied with the way he had ridden the trial, whether he ranged himself alongside Archer's accusers over St. Blaise's Derby, or whether the financial arrangements suggested by Archer were not to his liking, will never be known. At all events before the final breach between them came, in the autumn of this year, Archer rode only one more winner for Portland. This was in a little race at Langwell. So, as well as having lost Falmouth, his retainer and his rides, he was now in the process of losing Portland and St. Simon. What Archer thought of Portland has not been revealed, but we know his opinion of St. Simon. He said he was the best horse he ever rode. This, of course, was before the advent of Ormonde.

That was what he told a reporter who came down in March to discuss with him the prospects of the great sale and the coming season. 'What do you think Busybody will fetch?' the reporter also asked him.

'Mr. Dawson thinks she won't go under £8,000 or £10,000, and that Harvester ought to reach well over £5,000. He's improved very much, Harvester has; grown into a wonderfully

nice colt. That's what Mr. Dawson puts them down at—
15,000 guineas, I should say—for the pair.' This was to prove a
remarkably accurate forecast. He went on to say that he thought
he would ride Cambusmore for the Duke of Westminster in the
Derby, and that he had been seriously thinking of riding in that
year's Grand National.

'I should have ridden, no doubt, if Dog Fox had gone on
well and seemed to have a chance, but he has none and so it's no
use . . . but I shall very likely ride at Liverpool next year—if I
get the chance of a mount on something good enough, you
know! If I do ride I shall want to win!' He then gave a glimpse
of his state of mind by telling the newspaperman that he didn't
think he would be at the top of the tree on the flat in the coming
season. At all events he would not put himself about to do it.
His other interests were pressing upon him, his weight was
bothering him and he had been, after all, at the head of the list
for eleven years. He was to repeat these sentiments several times
to other reporters throughout the beginning of the year. It was
a time of crisis and change for him. He was noticeably worried
and unhappy. He kept repeating how much he would miss the
association with Lord Falmouth. 'You may be sure I am sorry to
think I am parting with the Wheel of Fortune jacket. I have
ridden for Lord Falmouth for twelve years and there has never
been a wrong word,' he told a reporter.

And indeed, outwardly at any rate, all was still on a friendly
basis between Falmouth, his trainer and his jockey. Before the
sale Dawson and Archer decided to make a presentation to him.
They bought a magnificent silver salver and had it engraved
with the names and dates of his Classic winners. There were, in
all, fourteen names on the salver. Of this impressive total all had
been trained by Mat Dawson and all save Kingcraft and Cecilia
ridden by Archer. It bore the following inscription: *Offered for
the acceptance of the Right Honourable Viscount Falmouth by his
trainer and jockey Mathew Dawson and Frederick J. Archer, as a
token of gratitude and esteem to the best, kindest and most generous
of masters on his retirement from the Turf, January 1884.*

[140]

Dawson also commissioned A. L. Townsend the sporting artist to paint a portrait of himself, Archer and Lord Falmouth with the string of horses around them. Ever afterwards this occupied a proud position amongst Dawson's pictures and Felix Leach who had joined the stable the previous year and who later became Dawson's assistant and later still made a name in his own right on the Turf, christened it 'The Last Muster'.

Before the sale something else happened. George Alexander Baird was reinstated. How this came about, stories differ. In the intervening period the Grand National Hunt Committee which had sentenced Baird had been disbanded 'for reasons which it is not necessary to go into here' according to the writer on steeple-chasing in the Badminton Library volume on racing, and a new Committee constituted. Some writers say that his reinstatement was automatic but it is probable that he had at least to make formal application. Charles Morton, who trained for him later on, says that Baird determined to make sure that there would be no hitch about his getting back and have his revenge on the authorities at the same time.

Hearing that the Limekilns at Newmarket then owned by a Mrs. Tharp were for sale he determined to buy them. The Stewards, he declared, would find themselves in a deucedly awkward position if the ownership of one of the best gallops at Newmarket passed into the hands of a man who was warned off the Turf. Even Morton, who was one of the few people with whom 'The Squire', as Baird was thenceforward usually called, shared any confidences, did not know what happened next. All he did know was that the Jockey Club took over the Limekilns and Baird's warning-off notice was revoked.

This time Baird determined to make a success of his career on the Turf and achieve his ambition of being the leading amateur rider of his day. As in earnest of all this he banished the spongers and riff-raff who hung around him, changed his colours from 'cardinal jacket and cambridge blue cap' to 'green jacket, plum cap' and decided to lay out a vast sum on purchasing the best bloodstock that money could buy.

Lord Falmouth's sale presented him with a splendid opportunity. It is said that he went through the catalogue with Archer and took his advice on what purchases to make. Whether he did or not, for once his money was not ill-spent. The horses in training were sold on the Monday of the first Spring Meeting at Newmarket. Baird's was the top price—8,800 guineas for Busybody. Harvester was runner-up, going to Sir John Willoughby for 8,600 guineas. The total for twenty-four lots was 36,440 guineas, but, with the exception of the two named, it must be said that not one of the others turned out a worthwhile purchase. With these two, the filly and the colt, went the Classic hopes of that year for Heath House.

Troubles now began to crowd upon Archer thick and fast. Rumours came to the ears of Sir George Chetwynd that a jockeys' ring was being operated, and that in control of this ring were Archer and Wood. Races were being fixed by these two, so the rumour said, and only horses chosen by them allowed to win. Sir George took it upon himself to call both of them before him and interview them. When they denied the accusations with some vehemence he told them that, though he accepted these denials, he feared that the rumours had received such publicity that only a full inquiry by the Jockey Club would clear their names. Without any consultation with the club or the Stewards he took the extraordinary course of inserting the following notice in the form of a question in the sheet calendar:

> *To ask the stewards whether they are aware that it is openly stated that a conspiracy exists between certain jockeys and so-called 'professional backers' of horses to arrange the result of races for their own benefit, and, if they have heard of such statements, and believe it possible such a plot exists, what steps they propose taking to deal with the matter at once.*

Naturally enough, the Stewards and the Jockey Club were not best pleased at this action by Sir George, especially since even then rumours were circulating as to the in and out form of Sir George's runners when ridden by Wood. They told him with some sharpness that they considered they had sufficient powers to deal with any of the matters raised by his question if a concrete case were put before them. One cannot but think that in this instance Sir George was using Archer's name and reputation as a shield behind which Wood, and to some degree himself, could shelter. In so far as Archer was concerned he was gratuitously dragged into a matter with which he had nothing to do and which should have never been raised. The unsatisfactory outcome caused him further worry and distress and served to raise about him another cloud of unfounded suspicion which should have been, but never was, satisfactorily dispersed.

Cambusmore, meanwhile, was out of the Classics. John Porter decided that he was too overgrown to have any chance and wanted more time to develop. So Archer had to look around again. Here, at first sight, he seemed fortunate, for his old friend Captain Machell had a strong hand that year. Sir John Willoughby had sent him Harvester, and in addition there was St. Medard, a small colt but full of quality, and a good filly by Hermit called Queen Adelaide in Machell's care.

At the Guineas Meeting the Duchess of Montrose announced in public what she had already said privately, that she would continue to race her own and her late husband's horses under the *nom de course* of Mr. Manton, the name being derived from Alec Taylor's training quarters, and that Archer would ride for her whenever possible.

There was a lavish breakfast party at Falmouth House on the morning of the Two Thousand. Champagne flowed and the guests made the most of it. Archer had elected to ride St. Medard and one of the guests asked him what his chances were, adding that he had backed St. Medard and Royal Fern.

'They'll both run well, I expect, but I think Scot Free is sure to beat them,' Archer said. 'You'd better back him whatever else you've done.'

Scot Free won easily from St. Medard who just beat Harvester by a neck for a second place. Mr. John Foy, the colt's owner, had originally engaged Fordham to ride Scot Free. But his years and

[143]

his former way of life had told on Fordham. He decided that he could not go on riding and, shortly before the meeting, he announced his retirement from the saddle. So this very great rider, perhaps the only one ever to be Archer's master, missed making his final ride a winning one in a classic race and defeating his old rival for the last time.

Busybody duly won the One Thousand Guineas for Baird, so a considerable amount of her purchase money was immediately recovered but, since he did not ride her, Archer must have bitterly regretted her sale and the loss of adding another Classic to his record. Worse was to come. Machell gave him his choice of his three entries for the Derby—Queen Adelaide, Harvester or St. Medard. He had plenty of opportunity to make up his mind for he was constantly at Machell's, dining with him and discussing the horses. Shortly before Derby Day he rode in a gallop in which all three went. He decided that St. Medard was the most likely to act on the course and that he would ride him. St. Medard was well beaten by both of the others. Harvester dead-heated for first place and Queen Adelaide was third. He had made the wrong choice, and the pick of Lord Falmouth's string had confirmed their two-year-old promise by winning two of the first three Classics—but not for Archer or Heath House. Then Busybody rubbed in the disaster of the sale by winning the Oaks, and once more Archer could not ride her.

These reverses put him on his mettle again. Now that he was back in the thick of things the resolve to take racing more easily was long forgotten. At one period Wood looked like overhauling him in the list. His competitive nature came to the fore and drove him on. Once more he was riding here, there and everywhere, to maintain his lead and to make up his losses.

At Ascot the luck began to swing his way again. Lord Hastings had in Melton, a two-year-old by Master Kildare, a colt of very high quality indeed. Mat Dawson introduced him to racing that Royal Ascot and in Archer's hands he won the New Stakes in style. Dawson was doubly pleased by this victory for he had always believed in the potentialities of Master Kildare as a sire and had encouraged Lord Hastings to use him. Very few others agreed with him, the horse was neglected and in his first year only got three foals, all the property of Lord Hastings. Two were colts, one a filly. The better looking of the two colts was christened Melton after his owner's home at Melton Constable in Norfolk. Dawson divined Melton's promise from the moment he came into his care, but on this occasion neither he nor Archer believed the colt to be quite ready. The manner of his victory and its ease surprised them and they realized that if all went well they had here a very live candidate for next year's Derby.

At Ascot, too, Archer won the Wokingham with Energy and the Alexandra Plate on Corrie Roy, both for the Duchess; but he did not have the mount on St. Simon in the Gold Cup. That honour went to Wood who rode St. Simon in all his four starts and four victories as a three-year-old. The financial rewards of racing St. Simon as a three-year-old when he was not in the Classics proving meagre, Portland, who did not bet, decided to retire him to stud so that he did not race after this season. He left the Turf unbeaten and indeed all but unchallenged. It is impossible to say how good he was, but he was to prove as great a sire as he was on the racecourse.

On the Monday of the July Newmarket Meeting the remainder of Lord Falmouth's stud, yearlings, brood mares and stallions came up for sale. Of the mares Spinaway fetched 5,500 guineas, Wheel of Fortune, 5,000 and Jannette 4,200; Gaillard made top price of the stallions at 3,600 guineas and the final total when added to that of the horses in training came to the impressive sum of 111,880 guineas. It may well have been that Lord Falmouth's luck and the blood of his mares and stallions had run out at the same time and that he displayed wisdom in selling. Of the entire lots that came under the hammer only Harvester and Busybody repaid their purchasers. A sporting writer later analysed the histories of all the animals sold and declared that the whole stud would have been dear at £50,000.

Archer then won the Stewards Cup at Brighton with Brag

behind whom there was now no Fordham to upset and confuse him, the Yorkshire Oaks with Clochette, who had led St. Simon in his first trial, and a host of other races. At Thirsk the Town Crier went through the streets proclaiming him 'The Wonder of the World' and advertising his presence at the races. The Duke of Westminster claimed him for Cambusmore in the St. Leger. Porter had thought that Cambusmore might be coming to hand for he had won the St. James's Palace Stakes at Ascot, but he ran badly and finished nowhere.

Melton was in the Middle Park Plate, the two-year-old Derby, for which Dawson and Archer had been quietly getting him ready. Their great rival Porter thought, however, that he might have a rod in pickle for them in that race.

In the summer of 1883 Porter and Captain Bowling had gone to the Yardley Stud to run their eyes over the yearlings that were to come up for sale. There they saw a big rangy colt by Casuistry. He was no beauty but Porter's experienced eye and flair told him that here was a racehorse in the making. Unable to go to the sale himself he instructed Tom Jennings to make sure of getting the colt. Jennings bought him for £700 and Porter and Bowling became his joint owners. Subsequently Bowling bought out Porter's share. Porter always believed in giving his horses time and it was not until 3rd October of the following year that he tried the colt who was still unnamed. Over five furlongs he beat four of Porter's good trial horses easily. They decided to call him Paradox and to run him in the Middle Park Plate.

The Duke of Westminster, whose sharp eyes had already picked out Paradox in his work, asked Bowling if he would sell. Bowling said he would—at £6,000. The Duke gave him this sum so that Bowling had a nice profit on his purchase.

In the Middle Park Paradox dwelt at the start and lost ground. Even so he dead-heated for third place, only two lengths behind the winner—Melton with Archer on his back.

Paradox had not grown any more handsome in the year since Porter had purchased him. Some of Westminster's friends laughed at him for owning such an ugly brute and there was a good deal of uninformed and adverse Press comment. One paper remarked that 'the backers of the Duke of Westminster's new purchase in the Middle Park Plate call it "the casualty colt".' Put out by all this, and for once not heeding Porter's advice, the Duke decided to get rid of Paradox. Porter had been better able to judge the running than most of the critics in the stand, and he did not wish to lose the colt. He prevailed on Mr. Broderick Cloete, a newcomer to the stable, to buy Paradox. Cloete, who was a businessman, said that if the Duke wanted so badly to be rid of him he must take a smaller price than he had given. They settled on £5,000 and Westminster was glad enough to see him go.

Archer and Melton went on to win the Criterion and establish Melton as the winter favourite for the Derby. But Melton was not engaged in the Dewhurst Plate whereas Paradox was. Porter secured Archer for the colt and they won it decisively, beating a high-class field. What Westminster said or thought has not been recorded. But Porter's judgement was vindicated once again; Archer now knew that he had two very live Classic candidates at his disposal for next season; and it was indeed a pleasant change of circumstances to win on a good horse that had been underrated rather than to be beaten on a moderate one that had been consistently overpraised.

So, with the three big back-end two-year-old races under his belt, the thanks of grateful owners and trainers in his ears and large presents in his bank account, things seemed to be coming his way again. Moreover, the number of winners he was to ride that year looked like turning into a truly formidable total. He was now over the two hundred mark and well ahead of Wood.

Then came the Cambridgeshire Week and more and bitter troubles. First, on the Monday there was a row and a bad one with John Hammond over the riding of Polaris. Hammond, who had won that year's Derby with Harvester, had started life as a stable boy with Captain Machell. Some of the Captain's astuteness had rubbed off on him and he was now a very successful owner and a tremendous gambler. Archer had ridden Polaris in other races and assumed that he would ride him at Newmarket. But Hammond, for reasons best known to himself but which may have had something to do with the contraction of the odds if Archer rode, stood him down. Polaris won without Archer's assistance and without his having been cut in on the coup. Hammond was known to have had £5,000 on and to have won a staggering figure. Hard words passed between them and, worse still, the Press got hold of the affair and played it up. After that, in the Cambridgeshire itself, Hammond rubbed salt into the wound by getting Webb to ride Florence who started joint favourite with Archer's mount Archiduc. Florence won by a head from Bendigo and Archer could only finish fourth. This enabled Hammond to pull off another immense gamble. Then Archer came under fire from the Press, especially the *Morning Post* who launched an extraordinary and apparently completely misconceived attack upon him over his riding of Energy and its running. He was said to be contemplating a libel action and that Lord Falmouth was backing him. Neither of the statements was accurate although it would seem from a study of the form that he could have sued had he so wished.

Unfortunately for him his name was always news. Now the fictitious affair of the 'Jockeys' Ring' to which Chetwynd had so unwisely given publicity earlier in the season, was dragged up again with his name coupled to it. *The supposed existence of planned frauds and robberies, the pulling of certain horses, the combination of certain jockeys are all tearing, so to speak, at the vitals of the Turf,* wrote *The World*, and the same paper pointedly continued: *Lord Falmouth may not know it, or he may shut his eyes and ears to what is going on, but I am only speaking the truth when I say that when three or four racing men are gathered together these are the comments made.*

The facts behind all this talk and rumour appear to be as follows: For a short time at this period of his life Archer was acting as adviser to a betting syndicate. Certain races were, on Archer's advice, selected by this syndicate for betting coups. In them

Archer would pick out a horse to ride which appeared to him to have an outstanding chance. When this had been done a suggestion would be made to certain of the other owners who were known to be approachable that it would profit all concerned were Archer's mount to win. There was no question of a far-reaching 'jockeys' ring' or anything like it, and obviously it was only on a few and carefully selected occasions that this scheme could be and was put into practice. Its success depended entirely on Archer's ability to assess form for it was never possible to eliminate the entire field. He had to be accurate in summing up just which horses represented dangers to him and what races should be chosen for the coups. It is a tribute to his skill in the saddle and his encyclopaedic knowledge of the form and running of the season's horses that he was usually right and until internal disagreements split the syndicate a considerable amount of money was amassed by it.

The rules of racing were then much more loosely interpreted than now and when one considers the conduct of one such as Chetwynd, a steward of the Jockey Club, which, until his fall, was largely condoned by his fellows it is not surprising that Archer, to say the least of it, saw nothing out of place in acting as he did in this matter.

But, as usual, worry and adverse publicity made him upset and miserable. Moreover he had cause for disquiet at home, too, for Nellie was pregnant again, her time was not far off and he had been warned that the confinement might be a difficult one.

And then, to cap it all, came the final parting with Portland.

'Abingdon' Baird had always hero-worshipped Archer. Now that he was back on the Turf and a reformed character, so he said and, for the moment, he did appear to be, the notion came to him that he and Archer should set up a joint racing establishment at Newmarket the following year. He approached the jockey with the proposition. Whether Archer ever seriously considered it is not known but news of the suggestion leaked out and came to the ears of Portland.

Baird's name was anathema to the authorities of the day.

Portland had ambitions at Court—he was to be made Master of the Horse in 1886—and probably for preferment in the counsels of the Jockey Club. These ambitions may have prompted him to act as he did. It is said that he sent for Archer and peremptorily told him that he objected to any jockey of his having an arrangement with Baird, that he understood Archer had come to such an arrangement and that he must either sever it or cease to ride in Portland's colours. These were strong words. Coming as they did from a pillar of the ruling few, one of the richest men on the Turf and a power in the all-but feudal society of the day, they might have intimidated a lesser man. But Archer never took kindly to being bullied. He knew his value and he had his pride. He was a temperamental man at the peak of a great profession. He rejected the ultimatum, and told Portland in terms as blunt as had been used to him that he reserved to himself the right to pick his own friends without interference from anyone however highly placed. The next day, in the picturesque phrase of the times, he 'sent back his cap and jacket', to Portland and also returned the balance of his retainer. A letter from Portland dated 21st October acknowledging this sum—£400—with an admission that it was 'very honourable' of Archer to return it is still extant and in print.

Portland was, however, unused to such rebuffs at the hands of a professional jockey and it was widely said at the time that he attempted to prevail upon Hastings, his partner in Archer's retainer, to take a similar course to his own. This Hastings refused to do. Since Falmouth had retired and Portland cut adrift, Hastings was now left with first claim on Archer's services. As things turned out it was fortunate indeed for Hastings that he endorsed neither Portland's sentiments nor his action.

After all this Archer went to Liverpool to ride Thebais in the Autumn Cup for the Duchess of Montrose. Thebais came home a winner at 5–2. His total was now 241. There was a fortnight of the flat season left; Wood was far behind; it looked as if with any luck he would set up such a record of wins as would stand for many years if not for ever. Fortune, perhaps, had started to smile again. For the moment the storms and upsets of the past few weeks were forgotten. He was pleased and happy. He liked riding winners for the old Duchess. Her open adoration was flattering and her presents lavish. 'Don't flirt with the Duchess,' one of the swells warned him in a letter when sending on the balance of a loan.

When he came back to the weighing-room he was given a telegram saying that Helen Rose had had a daughter and that all was well. On the train back to Newmarket he, for once, reflected how lucky he was. His wife and child were well, the season, in the end, had turned out far better than he had expected, indeed, remembering the magnificent number of wins he indulged himself in the luxury of describing it as a 'brilliant' one; the row with Portland really did not matter for there were Melton and Paradox to be ridden in the next year's Classics, neither of which belonged to him; the loss of Lord Falmouth's horses had not hampered him in amassing this year's huge total. Life, in fact, just at the moment, rows and scandals forgotten, looked very good.

When he returned to Falmouth House all still seemed well. His sister, Mrs. Coleman, had come down to look after Nellie and had everything in her charge. He thought he would hunt with the Drag the next day. Before he set out, he decided, he would go in to see his wife in his hunting clothes for she always said he looked his best in them. He was turning over in his mind the pleasure this would give her when suddenly there was commotion. Mrs. Coleman rushed into the room calling that Nellie was dying. Together they ran to his wife's bedside. She was in convulsions and died in agony without recognizing him.

Chapter 10

His friends did not think he would ever recover. He was completely broken up. It was only after it happened that those about him realized the depth of his affection for Helen Rose. Always inclined to melancholy, that side of his temperament purged and kept at bay only by violent action, now he became almost maniac. He could not sleep. Sunk in a gloom, he would talk to no one. Racing was, of course, out of the question, but he would not go out to look at the Heath House horses or to supervise his own yard. Sitting all day in a chair, hollow-eyed from lack of sleep, he stared into space. Once or twice he spoke of suicide. Captain Bowling came down to stay but he could do nothing to help his friend to lift himself out of the trough of his depression.

Finally Captain Bowling and Mrs. Coleman decided that something must be done. They put it to Archer that in his own interests and those of the child, he must try to recover and to go on with his life. They suggested that he should go away on a trip. Captain Bowling advised America where there was no language difficulty and there were plenty of friends and acquaintances. He consented and, having done so, drove himself into activity. At first he wanted Herbert Mills, his old Cheltenham friend to accompany him but when business interests prevented this he asked Bowling. Bowling agreed, indeed it is almost certain he all along intended to go, and began to make the arrangements. There was much to be done. Plans had to be made, passages booked and all the multitude of wires and letters of sympathy from the highest to the lowest in the land to be acknowledged and answered. The Prince of Wales had sent a telegram, so had Lord Falmouth and the Duke of St. Albans. There was a gushing wire from the Duchess, a cold and formal note from Portland and a warm and friendly letter from Rosebery. When the Duchess heard of the proposed trip she despatched letters of introduction couched in the warmest terms to her American friends; Rosebery wrote to Mr. Belmont, President of the American Jockey Club, on his behalf, recommended him to a hotel, *The Brevoort House, small and quiet and kept by Mr. Waite. If you told him you came from me I am sure he would make you comfortable.* He also advised him to take plenty of warm clothing.

Then there was the matter of his will to be attended to. The child must be provided for since no one knew what would happen on an extended trip of this sort. He went off to Cheltenham in a hurry, walked into the office of Jessop, his solicitor, gave him rough instructions and told him to have the will ready for signature that afternoon. The solicitor protested that his instructions were too vague and the time too short to allow him to prepare the will as he would have liked. He made a good job of it just the same. Robert Herbert Mills, his old friend, was one executor and Archer's brother-in-law, George Peddie Thomas Dawson, the other. After providing a trust fund for his father and mother and making certain bequests including ' £1,000 to my valet, William Bartholomew, generally known as Solomon', the bulk of the estate went to the daughter.

Jessop and his clerk witnessed the will and Jessop told him again that it was all done in too much of a hurry but that at least he should nominate guardians for the daughter in case of a minority. Archer agreed to this and with great difficulty, for he had still not entirely mastered the business of handwriting, he took a sheet of Jessop's paper and wrote and signed a direction that the Dawsons should have care of the child. Jessop said afterwards that these directions were the only handwriting of Archer's save for his signature that he ever had.

[153]

On 15th November Archer, Bowling and the valet, Solomon, embarked at Queenstown, Ireland, for America in the *Bothnia*. The journey was uneventful and they made a fast passage, reaching New York on 20th November. Archer's first act on arrival was to cable and inquire about the infant daughter. The answer came that she was healthy and flourishing. Then, relieved of immediate anxieties on that score, he was free to turn his attentions to the New World.

His fame was, of course, now far larger than the mere coterie reputation of a racing figure. Reporters, forewarned of his coming, poured on board immediately the ship docked. American newspapermen who covered arrivals from ocean-going liners were a hard-boiled lot quick to scent out pretension, and to puncture it, ready to snap back at any show of patronage towards their city or their nation. But they took to Archer immediately, liking him for his quietness and quick wit, his complete absence of conceit or stuffiness.

With Captain Bowling hovering anxiously in the background like some rather lugubrious shade, he answered the drumfire of questions as if he had been doing it all his life. No, he would not ride any races during his stay. 'Please say I would not ride a race during this trip for £5,000.' His most sensational victory? The Derby on Bend Or. 'It was right out of the fire I can tell you, sir.' American horses? 'First class. I found Iroquois a magnificent animal, kind, willing and gentle. Foxhall was another good one and his Cambridgeshire victory with 126 lb. up, was a tall performance.' Parole? 'A good handicap animal but not really tiptop. I rode him a winner and was glad of it.'

These were the sort of answers they liked. Archer, as usual, was off to a good start.

They did not, as it happened, stay at the hotel recommended by Lord Rosebery but at the Brunswick on Fifth Avenue. They were entertained by Governor Vanderbilt and fêted wherever they went. But Archer was determined to keep away from racing and the racecourse, to forget his former life, at least for the present, utterly and completely. He had come as a tourist and as

such he would remain, travelling all the time, always in move-
ment, on the go, trying by means of new sights and sounds and
meeting fresh people from milieus and backgrounds he had
never known before to kill the pain of his loss and to fill the
emptiness within him. He did not entirely succeed. His friends
maintained and indeed he said himself that he was never the
same man again, but at least he freed himself from the blackness
of his early despair.

After he had seen New Orleans he went on a shooting trip
into the wilds living rough for five weeks and liking it. He
visited Washington, Niagara, the stockyards of Chicago, where
Solomon contracted a fever and had to be sent home, then went
once more south to St. Louis, Houston, Texas, and Florida. He
was in Canada, too, and thought the Windsor Hotel, Montreal,
the best of his trip. After that he came back to New York for
the final weeks of his stay. A hack through Central Park in
company with William Easton, an American bloodstock auc-
tioneer, on a thoroughbred stallion called Pet Bud was the only
time he sat on a horse during the entire trip.

Celebrities, as always, pursued him; as always he avoided
their attentions. He did, however, pay a visit to the Tombs
where Miss Dudley was being held in what he considered to be
very comfortable detention after her attempt to shoot O'Donovan Rossa. She told him she next intended to come to England
and shoot Gladstone and then she would join the Mahdi. He
thought her one of the finest-looking women he ever saw. He
missed his train to Kentucky and had to abandon a visit to Mr.
Lorillard's stud-farms and the Blue-grass country. And then it
was time to board the *Bothnia* for the journey back.

It took longer than they had expected owing to the ship running into bad weather in mid-Atlantic and as a result he could
not come back through Ireland and call on Mr. Linde. It was 9th
March when he landed at Liverpool and there was not much
time to get ready for the coming season.

For he had now no intention of giving up riding. 'I am so
thoroughly wrapped up in racing,' he had told Mr. Easton dur-

ing that ride in Central Park, 'my mind is so entirely upon it, that I really never think of anything else, not even of where I am and of what is going on around me as I travel about from place to place.'

There was no question but that the change of scene and surroundings, the bustle and flurry and varied interests of the trip had done him a world of good. In appearance he looked far healthier, though his friends noticed that there were lines of care now etched on to his face which had not been there before and which were never to leave him. Physically, he had filled out— too much, indeed, for his immediate purposes since he turned the scale at 9 st. 10 lb. After giving his impressions of the trip to the English pressmen he left immediately for Newmarket, bringing with him an American basket-work perambulator for the child. The Dawsons and Mrs. Coleman gave him reassuring news of her. Straight away he went back to the arduous routine of fasting, Turkish baths and purgations.

The great house which he had so proudly built for himself and his bride and upon which he had lavished so much care and money was empty and lonely. Racing was the only way of life he knew. To devote all his thoughts and energies and every waking moment to the business of riding winners and still more winners, his only anodyne.

His first work was ridden on Toastmaster, one of Dawson's Lincoln entries, and his first ride in public was on Mr. F. Robinson's Laceman at the Lincoln Meeting, where he was placed third.

The crowd greeted the reappearance of their favourite with a storm of cheers. The cheaper rings took it up and as he cantered down to the start roar upon roar of cheering followed him to below the distance. It was a hero's return and a hero's welcome. Immediately he set out to justify it.

Chapter 11

❦

Melton and Paradox had both wintered well though it is said that Dawson was never entirely happy about the soundness of Melton's legs, and was careful never to overwork or over-race him. Melton did not run in the Two Thousand Guineas which left Archer free for Paradox.

On 30th April Porter tried Paradox with four others, Whipper-In, a six-year-old; Cambusmore, Farewell and Metal. Farewell was fancied for the One Thousand and Porter wanted to see how both of them went. Paradox had 9 st. 7 lb. on his back and was giving the filly 21 lb. He won the trial unextended, by half a length. Farewell, getting lumps of weight all round, finished fourth. Porter reckoned that he would win the Two Thousand but that his chances with the filly were slight.

In the Guineas Paradox started at 3–1 on. Good colt though he was, Paradox was an exceedingly difficult racehorse on which to win races. The basis of the trouble was that he would not race when in front. Once he saw daylight he would drop his bit and cease to try unless he had on his back someone with the hands and strength and touch to persuade him to run on. Archer, having ridden him at home and on the racecourse, knew of his peculiarities. But so did Tom Cannon. Like Archer, Cannon lived for racing and nothing else; like Archer, too, he used his eyes and his brains. He had ridden against Paradox, guessed at his weakness and thought he knew a way to beat him. Cannon was engaged to ride Mr. Gerard's Crafton in the race; the field was a distinctly moderate one and this helped Cannon's plans.

Despite all he could do, at the Dip, Archer was left in front. This was what Cannon had counted upon. He sat behind Paradox, sure that he would shorten his stride when in front on the hill, and that he could come with one run and beat him. Unfortunately for Cannon he had Archer to beat as well and Cannon, with all his ability, had not quite the genius of Fordham.

Somehow Archer persuaded Paradox to keep on racing. He even slightly increased his lead. Baffled, Cannon came out to make his run. For once he had left it a shade too late, let the other get just too far away. With Crafton creeping up beside him Paradox caught hold of his bit and stretched his neck. Archer kept him going. He won by a head.

Very few, even among the knowledgeable, knew of Paradox's peculiarities for, naturally enough, Porter and the Kingsclere staff were at some pains to keep them secret. Even Sir George Chetwynd was deceived into blaming Archer. Wood, who was on the third horse, came in and told Sir George that Archer had ridden a bad race and that Paradox was sure to win the Derby. Wood's word was gospel to Sir George at that time and, in fact, he never learnt of Paradox's manner of running or, if he did, he never admitted his mistake. The general public, too, accepted that Paradox had been badly ridden and it even began to be said in some quarters that Archer was not the man he had been. Paradox's merits were certainly underlined when Farewell won the One Thousand Guineas. Then Melton made his first appearance of the season in the Payne Stakes at Epsom. This was to be his only race before the Derby. With Archer in the saddle and looking a picture he beat his three opponents with majestic ease.

The Derby rivalry was now becoming acute. As the days passed the riding arrangements had to be finalized. Melton remained sound. Dawson exercised Lord Hastings's first claim on Archer. Though he could do nothing about this and must indeed have anticipated it, Porter was dismayed. Archer knew all about

Paradox's ways of running, he had the brains to think up a scheme to beat him and the ability to put it into practice. This, in fact, was just what he was doing. But he himself was worried about Crafton. Remembering the Guineas, he told his friends that if Tom Cannon rode Crafton he might beat them both.

Cannon, however, was claimed by Lord Rosebery and Watts engaged for Crafton. Porter booked Fred Webb for Paradox and briefed him carefully about the horse's peculiarities and the dangers represented by Archer.

Intense interest and excitement were aroused by this Derby, and the meeting of these two great colts. Rumours of nobbling and that Webb was to be got at flew about and Paradox drifted in the betting to 6–1. Melton was a firm favourite at 75–40.

Before Webb went out to ride Mr. Cloete told him that if he had been offered anything to throw the race he would double it if he won. Then he went even further and told Porter and Webb that they could divide the stake between them. Porter commented afterwards that Webb had an unenviable task before him when he went out and he was right.

The Prince and Princess of Wales and their family were in the Royal Box along with a bevy of other Princes and Royalty. The Duke of Westminster was with them as was Portland who was now beginning to make his way at Court; he did not have a runner and may well have watched with mixed feelings Archer mounting his friend's colt. Lord Hastings himself was on the stand but unaccompanied by his wife who had borne him a son only a fortnight before. Rosebery had come across from the Durdans, and Chetwynd, of course, was in the paddock running his knowledgeable eye over the field. He had heard rumours about Melton's legs and had a commission to lay against him. But when he saw the colt stripped he said to his trainer: 'I wish all my racehorses were shaped like him.' *The beau ideal of a racehorse*, he wrote later. *A whole-coloured bay, on the small side with wonderful back and quarters and perfect shoulders and action. No lumber, no trouble to train, perfect and symmetrical in all points.*

In fact the business of Melton's legs is extraordinary. The

touts all had it that he had a 'bowed sinew'. Many of the news-papers said that he would not stand training and, when he did, heaped praise on Mat Dawson for his skill. But none of the Turf historians mention the fact and Chetwynd, having looked at him closely, appears to have discounted the stories. Even after the race they persisted and were current up to the St. Leger. But Melton, although this is anticipating, went on to a strenuous programme as a four-year-old. His temperament deteriorated, but his legs do not appear to have interfered in any way with his racing career.

Beside Melton Paradox looked tough and clumsy. In a way it was Bend Or and Robert the Devil all over again.

Custance started them for the first time that year and, for once in his life, Archer was content to get off nearly last. Nor did he bustle Melton to take up a good position on the hill. He was intent upon seeing that Paradox was somehow left in front to make his own running, determined to do to Webb what Cannon had so nearly done to him. As usually happened when he had thought things out, the race was run exactly as he wanted it.

None of the other colts could live with Paradox. In the straight he was well clear of his field and looked like coming home alone. Then, there being nothing near him to race with, he began to drop his bit.

Archer on Melton had been steadily making up ground. The gap between the two horses began to close. Melton crept closer as Paradox shortened his stride and began to look all about him. Archer, his eyes on Paradox, watching him, timing his effort, still did not move.

When the horses were fifty yards from the post Archer pounced. The moment Paradox felt the other come up to him he commenced to run on again. Melton headed him. Paradox fought back and got in front once more. It was now or never. Archer went for his whip. He hit Melton twice. Perfectly timed, they were two tremendous strokes with everything he had in him behind them. Lord Rosebery said afterwards that he heard them on the stand. Melton shot forward. The post came up and fell back. No one could say which had won.

One of John Dawson's stable boys was lucky enough to be beside Paradox as Webb unsaddled him. 'I think I just got there,' he heard Webb say to Porter. Then the numbers went up and someone said: 'You're second, Fred.' Thirty years afterwards the boy could clearly remember the look on Webb's face when he heard those words. It was the fifth year in succession he had been placed in the Derby without winning it.

The crowd went wild with excitement. Archer was cheered and cheered again. The swells crowded around Lord Hastings with their congratulations. Well might he congratulate himself, too, on having sent his horses to Mat Dawson and having refused to part with Archer's services as a jockey. He rushed off to telegraph his wife: *Melton won a head Paradox second. Royal Hampton third. Had rather exciting moment.—Hastings Grand Stand Epsom.*

'Archer's Masterpiece' was how William Moorhouse, possibly the greatest Turf writer of all time, described this race. He was right and those most intimately concerned, including Mr. Cloete and Porter, knew it. 'There was probably no other jockey,' Porter wrote long afterwards, 'unless it was Tom Cannon, who could have got Paradox beaten in the Derby ... Webb rode a splendid race, and he would have done both himself and me a very good turn but for the masterful tactics, and the grim determination displayed by Archer.'

Nor were the Hastings slow in showing their gratitude. The present for his win was lavish in the extreme—half the stake of £4,525—and promptly paid. They tried to entertain him in their home but, as always, he refused to be lionized. He did, however, pay them a private visit at Melton Constable. Lady Hastings, who was still convalescing, secured her husband's permission to receive Archer in her room. He came up bringing with him the whip he had used in the race as a present for her. She was a pretty and vivacious creature and passionately interested in racing. She wanted to hear every detail of the running and he went over it for her again and again. Before he left, the

L　　　　　　　[161]

baby, dressed in the Hastings' colours of *eau-de-Nil* and crimson, was brought down to see him.

Both the Hastings were popular in Society and out of it and deservedly so, for they were a natural and unassuming couple. They had broader and more cultured interests than most of their kind and one of the many congratulatory telegrams to come to them after the race was from Oscar Wilde, not perhaps one of the most enthusiastic followers of racing or any other sport. It read: *I understand that Milton's 'Paradise Lost' is being revived and will appear in Derby Week and will be published under the title 'Paradox Lost' by Melton.* Neither of them ever forgot Archer or what they owed to him. Hastings did his best to overcome the barrier of class which lay between them and to make friends with the jockey as a man. To some extent he succeeded and Archer certainly admitted him more to his intimacy than the others of his noble owners. Both of the Hastings remained devoted to him for the rest of his short life and to his memory long afterwards.

As if he had not had triumphs enough that week Archer went on to win the Oaks for Lord Cadogan on Lonely. Then Porter decided to send Paradox to Paris for the Grand Prix and asked Archer to ride him. They coasted home easy winners from Reluisant who had won the Prix du Jockey Club. This was some consolation to Porter and Mr. Cloete for their Derby defeat; the stake £5,504 being in fact greater than that at Epsom. Three of the four Classics were now Archer's, together with one of the French Classics and a truly astounding total of wins. And the season was not yet half-way through.

Fordham having gone, they were calling Archer 'the demon' instead of him and, indeed, that wonderful season, there was something almost demonic in his manner of riding. He had to win. It was, at this time, everything he lived for. There were no distractions. The child was being well looked after by the Dawsons. There was nothing to come home to. He could not return to his spartan rooms at Heath House and his own mansion was gaunt and unlived in without the presence of Nellie Rose. He wasted more and more to do ridiculous weights for his tall frame and to ride winners and yet more winners.

The company of the old Duchess was some sort of spurious consolation. From her headquarters at Sefton Lodge she was now really in full sail after him. She was a ruthless woman and she usually got what she wanted. Letters, invitations, telegrams, offers to ride, flew from her pen. Generous and charming when she wanted to be and given to the grand gesture—she had cancelled all her runners on the day of Nellie Rose's funeral—there was no denying she could be good company. He liked riding winners for her and he was flattered by her attentions. Whether there is any truth in the oft-repeated story that he asked Machell if he married her would he become a Duke it is impossible to say but Lord Rosebery, who was a shrewd observer, thought that he did have ideas in that direction and, in his loneliness and wretchedness when men act out of character, he might well have done. At all events if he took his problem to Mat Dawson, as it is also said that he did, the old trainer's reply may be apocryphal but it is certainly typical. 'Don't be a dom'd fule,' Dawson said.

However Archer managed to dissociate himself from her matrimonial intentions he achieved a remarkable feat in that she remained on adoring terms with him for the rest of his days and he helped with the training of Thebais to win the Gold Vase at Ascot at 11–2 in that year.

Brilliant as the beginning of the season had been that back-end was to be even better.

Although Robert Peck had retired from active training he still owned horses. His friendship with Archer deepened and strengthened after the death of Helen Rose. They were frequently together and Archer was on hand to ride and advise on Peck's horses, their abilities and where to place them. Indeed in some of them he had partnerships or shares which were not registered. That year Peck had a brilliant two-year-old, The Bard, which he owned in partnership with General Owen Williams in which Archer had no active interest and which was trained by General Williams's trainer, Gurry. Nevertheless Gurry, too, was not averse to taking Archer's advice and Archer rode the colt in work and discussed his prospects with his trainer and owners.

The Bard was almost like a smaller edition of Bend Or, a brilliant chestnut below average size, but beautifully made and with a tremendous turn of speed. Archer won the Hartington Plate at Manchester with him at odds of no less than 10–1 on. He followed this by winning the John of Gaunt at the same meeting at 5–1 on.

General Owen Williams, who was prominent amongst the Marlborough House set and was a few years later to play a leading part in the Tranby Croft scandal that ruined Sir William Gordon Cumming, was a member of the Jockey Club and a tremendous gambler, who, at the end of his days, had gone through almost all of his money; he was neither very clever nor very wise and after The Bard had won all of his sixteen races that season it was perhaps tempting providence for him to say that his colt would never be beaten. For the two-year-olds that year must have been just about the best in the history of the Turf.

However, before he could get down to the business of picking and choosing which colt he would ride in the great end-of-season two-year-old races Archer had the St. Leger on his hands. Through an oversight of Captain Bowling's in making his nominations Paradox was not in this race but Melton was. Mat Dawson used all his skill in preparing Lord Hastings's colt and he came to Doncaster with his suspect legs 'as clean as bars of silver' as one commentator said. He started at 95–40 on and simply toyed with his field, lying last for much of the way and then winning as he liked by six lengths. Isobar was second and the Oaks winner, Lonely, third.

Then it was time for the two-year-olds. John Porter had one he thought well up to the standard of his 'flyers' and since he proved to be all that and more so it is necessary to say something about his history.

Lily Agnes, a mare who had won twenty-one races during her career, was brought to the Eaton Stud to be mated with

Bend Or's sire Doncaster. When she was there the stud-groom suggested to the Duke of Westminster that he should buy her. After some hesitation and doubts about the matter, for Lily Agnes was not prepossessing in her looks, the Duke did buy her for £2,500 and two free subscriptions to Bend Or. She proved to be a wonderful bargain and more than offset his bad luck in selling Paradox. First she produced, by Doncaster, Farewell, the winner of the Two Thousand Guineas. Then she was put to Bend Or. By him, after a twelve months' pregnancy, she produced a foal with a mane already three inches long who stood so much over at the knee that the stud-groom thought he would never grow straight. This foal was Ormonde. He was sent to Kingsclere as a yearling and Porter took to him immediately even though the first thing he did was to throw out very bad splints under both his knees. Porter got rid of the splints by the application of a patent medicine in which he believed and which had been successful before with others of his good horses, but they set back Ormonde in his preparation and it was not until August that they tried him. Ormonde was nothing like ready to run but, giving Porter's old reliable trial horse, Whipper-In, no less than 12 lb he beat him comfortably. Since Whipper-In had never let the stable down in a trial and had been used as a yardstick to measure the ability of countless high-class horses, Porter knew that in Ormonde he had a real good one though, as he said himself, he did not yet realize just how good he was. He immediately set about getting him ready to run.

Ormonde was in the Middle Park Plate but so were two good colts and a useful filly—Minting, Saraband and Braw Lass, all of whom had done a fair amount of racing and come superlatively through their early tests. Porter decided not to risk Ormonde against them but to run him instead in a Post Sweepstakes over the Bretby course, the race immediately preceding the Middle Park. Archer was to ride him.

There were only two other runners in the Post Sweepstakes, a filly of the Duke of Portland's out of Mowerina who had won eight of her ten races, and the Duke of Hamilton's Warbler.

Ormonde had now grown to sixteen hands and since he may well have been the greatest racing machine—on the flat—the world has ever known it is worth while to allow his trainer to describe him:

'His quarters were exceptionally powerful and, though rather short, his neck was the most muscular I ever saw a thoroughbred possess. He had a good bone, beautifully-laid shoulders, a very strong back and rather straight hocks. Although in his slow paces he had not a very taking action, he was a free mover. There was immense propelling power behind the saddle. His ears were inclined to lop. The width of his head behind the ears was remarkable; I never came across another horse that showed this characteristic to such an extent. Ormonde had a most amicable disposition and was a wonderful "doer" and never gave us any trouble. He would eat anything the man (Marlow) who "did" him offered. Cakes, apples—everything seemed to be acceptable. When galloping he carried his head rather low....'

Modwena was made favourite at 6–5 on. Without being extended and in heavy going Ormonde beat her a length. This pleased Porter and impressed Archer who must, too, have taken some satisfaction in upsetting the odds laid on Portland's filly. Except amongst the knowing this victory attracted very little notice. The attention of the public was concentrated on the race for the Middle Park.

Before the Meeting all sorts of stories had been flying about. Saraband was in the care of Humphries who looked after Robert Peck's horses under Peck's and Archer's supervision, John Dawson trained Braw Lass and his brother Mat, Minting. Archer thus had first-hand knowledge of all three. Minting was a slashing big colt—'the best big horse I ever saw after Prince Charlie' was Sir George Chetwynd's comment. He won two races when ridden by Watts before Archer won the Champagne Stakes at Doncaster and the Triennial at Newmarket on him. Mat Dawson thought him as good as or better than any of his other Classic winners and that was saying something. But Braw Lass was getting 9 lb. from him and John Dawson thought a lot of Braw

Lass and Saraband had only been beaten once in seven starts. To add more fuel to the rumours that were flying around, the Duchess had St. Mirin in the race and was known to fancy it.

Although it was not Peck but Sir John Blundell Maple, a furniture millionaire who raced under the name of Mr. Childwick, who owned Saraband it was known that Peck was at least actively interested in the horse's fortunes. The all-prevalent rumour was that he and Archer had settled the race between them and that Archer would stop Minting to allow Saraband to win and thus recoup some of his gambling losses.

The running of the race made tongues wag even more furiously than they had done before. Braw Lass shot into a long lead and Archer, thinking she could not possibly stay the distance, let her go. It was one of his few bad mistakes and the Middle Park one of his few bad races. Coming into the Dip he realized that she had slipped him. Immediately he got at Minting. Big and overgrown, Minting, being sent about his business too suddenly, sprawled and became unbalanced. Wood on Saraband, seeing Archer make his effort, set his mount alight. He, too, looked to have left it too late. Braw Lass seemed a certain winner. As always, those who thought so reckoned without Archer.

Somehow he balanced Minting and made him race. It was one of his efforts that showed him as the genius he was. In the very last stride he got Minting up to win by a head. Braw Lass was second, Saraband a neck away third.

The wiseacres afterwards one and all maintained that it was only when he knew Saraband was beaten that Archer got at Minting. Mr. Vyner, Minting's owner, never even began to entertain the thought that this could be the truth nor did Mat Dawson. But it is important to note that when Archer came in he admitted he had ridden a bad race, but he went on to warn Dawson that from the way he had run he did not think Minting would act downhill and for this reason might not be a Derby horse.

After the Middle Park Archer won the Champion Stakes on Paradox, and then took both the Criterion and the Dewhurst with Ormonde, beating his friend the Duchess's Oberon in the first. These two important races were won with consummate ease despite the presence of good horses in their fields. Odds of no less than 6–4 and 11–4 were laid on Ormonde so that it was obvious the public were at last coming round to the realization of his potential. He was then put by for the winter watched over by the admiring and solicitous eye of Porter and his staff.

Unlike St. Simon, Ormonde, as befitted a son of Bend Or, was placid in his temperament and gave no trouble in his box or in the yard. They cared for him like the prince he was and in those winter months he grew, thickened and prospered.

Archer finished this wonderful season having won four Classics and 246 races out of 667 rides. It was the greatest number of winners he was ever to ride. That year, too, he had more mounts than ever before, a sign of a dedication to racing so complete that it excluded everything else.

The number of winning rides was a record. It was one which was to stand for forty-eight years until Gordon Richards beat it in 1933. By two extraordinary coincidences Richards equalled Archer's total on the anniversary of Archer's last ride and beat it on the anniversary of his death.

It is worth while to consider this astounding feat of Archer's a little more fully, and to examine the disadvantages which he had to overcome. In order to ride at all he had to subject himself to a health-destroying routine of wasting, and even when under the most drastic deprivations he had difficulty in doing eight stone eight. This, of necessity, limited the number of rides he could take and the number of possible winners available to him. He was uneducated and practically unable to put pen to paper yet he had no secretary nor any of the modern aids to communication such as the typewriter or the telephone. All his engagements had to be made by telegram, letter or personal contact, and, when made, carried in his head. The making of these arrangements alone involved constant travelling, coming and going, calling and meeting those who wanted to engage him. As if this was not enough for a champion jockey, he also had the responsibilities of a partnership in Heath House, one of the most important training establishments in the land, as well as owning or part owning horses all over the country and acting as adviser to their trainers or the owners of the other shares. No one knows how many or how great were the constant calls on his purse from his family and others whom he helped. He was, too, a heavy and unsuccessful gambler.

Besides all this he had his own temperament to contend with. Highly-strung, melancholic and sensitive, he was by nature singularly unfitted for the position in the limelight into which his genius drove him. Unfavourable public comments made in the Press or conveyed to him by trouble-making acquaintances, slander and back-biting such as it is almost inevitable for a man in his position to suffer, racked him mentally. Ill-equipped to stand up to private troubles he had far more than his fair share of them in the few short years during which his genius flared across the racecourses of Great Britain. The loss of his brother, his son and his wife in the space of seven years came upon him one after the other to take away the taste of his triumphs and leave bitterness and despair instead. Despite these blows he never succumbed to the temptations of the flesh freely offered him, or lowered his own high professional standards. He did not take to the bottle as Fordham did nor to malpractices as, unfortunately, was the case with Wood.

In the actual business of riding races he had vast distances to cover with none of the modern aids such as the motor-car or the aeroplane. His methods of transport were the horse and the railway with all the disadvantages, inconveniences and additional physical strain that came with them.

Those 246 winners were an all but incredible achievement. They were the summit and crown of his career. They brought him no happiness.

Chapter 12

That winter the racing world had much to talk about. Never before had there been such a plethora of talent for the coming season's Classics. Mat Dawson, usually the most non-committal and taciturn of men, made no secret that he thought Minting a world-beater; General Owen Williams, in his clubs—the Turf, the Yacht Squadron, the Marlborough and the Carlton; over dinner and baccarat tables with H.R.H. and his cronies, Val Baker of the 10th Hussars, Sporting Joe Aylesford, Louis de Rothschild and the like, was repeating his opinion that The Bard was unbeatable; the Duchess thought highly of St. Mirin, and Robert Peck was known to hold that in Saraband he had the winner of the next Two Thousand Guineas. And at Kingsclere John Porter was quietly watching Ormonde grow into greatness. Every single one of these owners and trainers wanted Archer to ride their crack for them. He took his time about making up his mind.

That winter, though he needed it badly, he could not rest. He was for ever on the go, watching the wintering of the Heath House horses, hunting with the Drag or in the shires with Custance, dining with Machell or Peck, advising them, talking ceaselessly and into the small hours about horses and racing. At his elbow was the sombre figure of Captain Bowling, devoted, lugubrious, doing his best to look after Archer's affairs, to help him in his business dealings and to cope with the mass of correspondence, begging letters and anonymous abuse, and keep at bay the sightseers and hangers-on that converged on Archer wherever he went.

That winter, too, something else happened which vitally affected Archer's life. Throughout the previous season Dawson had been seriously considering the idea of retirement. He was now sixty-five years of age and, where his horses were concerned, he had always been a worrier and a perfectionist. The strain of running a large stable for noble, demanding and wealthy owners was beginning to tell on him. His nephew George had been having trouble with his health and, through illness, had given up his job in Burton as a brewer. At Ascot that year Dawson had a discussion with him as a result of which George took up residence at Heath House for a trial period of six months to see if he could take over the stable. By Goodwood Mat had decided that George would do. During the Meeting he finally made up his mind to go. He asked an old friend and benefactor, Sir John Don-Wauchope, to write down at his dictation a simple surrender of his tenancy in Heath House and an instruction that this was to be assigned to his principal owners, the Duke of Portland and Lord Hastings, at the end of the season. When the time came Portland and Hastings asked Lord Londonderry and Lord Crewe to join them in partnership and the four noblemen, on the recommendation of Mat, appointed George Dawson as their private trainer. It does not appear that Mat's partnership with Archer was ever formally dissolved.

Leaving Felix Leach behind him for two years to help young George find his feet Mat moved to Exning Manor House bringing with him a few horses of his own, the one or two that Lord Falmouth had still in training and those belonging to Mr. Vyner amongst whom was Minting.

Exning Manor House appeared to Dawson to be rather a grand address for the attractive but unpretentious residence he had bought so he renamed it Melton House and there he settled down in semi-retirement. Although he had left Newmarket his friendship with Archer, forged as it had been by the years of greatness and success, did not entirely lapse. Every week-end

Archer would travel to Exning to ride out on Dawson's horses and advise him as he had always done. 'Throw your leg over that big fellow, Fred, and see what he is,' were Dawson's instructions when they were wondering how Minting had wintered. Archer rode Minting out and told Dawson not to think too much of him or of his chances of beating Ormonde which warnings Dawson disregarded, to his cost as we shall see.

It was, however, unlikely that any consortium of owners headed by Portland would look very kindly on a close association with Archer and thus, after all the years, the ties which bound him to Heath House were loosened and finally severed. There were new faces there now and different men in command. He was free to go elsewhere and he did.

When the season of 1886 commenced Archer was not a well man. The year before he had returned from America at least physically refreshed. Then, too, he had to some extent at least been carried along by the tide of public adulation and by his tremendous run of successes. Now he had no such respite behind him as he had been given by the American trip. Grief, physical strain, privations, mental torment were all taking their inevitable toll. He had been wasting now for thirteen years. Each season it grew harder to do the weight, each season the torture had to increase, the deprivations and purgations become more intense. Once the routine started the sight of food sickened him. He looked ghastly and his friends told him so. He took no notice. His only object in life was to ride winners and to ride winners he had to do the weight. It was as simple as that. There was nothing else to live for.

Immediately there was the business of deciding which colt he should ride in the Classics. Here was only one of the many occasions where he was to miss the immediate availability of Mat Dawson's kindly counsel. His retainers were by now in such confusion that at this distance of time it is quite impossible to sort them out. It is certain, however, that Sir Blundell Maple came along and offered him an enormous sum to ride Saraband in the Two Thousand and the Derby. As usual he needed the money. His betting had gone badly the year before and he was now speculating even more heavily. Either Porter and the Duke of Westminster had by now surrendered their claim or else they very sportingly agreed to let him go. Falmouth and Portland had gone. Perhaps Mat Dawson for once, did not want to enforce any claim if indeed he had one beyond the ties of friendship, for he was wildly over-confident, despite Archer's warnings, that he had in Minting the horse of the century.

At all events, it was eventually settled that Archer would ride Saraband in the Guineas and the Derby. It was an extraordinary decision for him to make seeing that Ormonde was in the race and opposed to him. It is impossible to say why he made it but one is entitled to guess that it was a mixture of the enticement of the money which he needed to recoup his gambling losses together with his friendship for Peck. However, decide he did. He would ride Saraband.

Porter had watched Ormonde wintering and in his early work that spring and knew now that in him he had a wonder. So sure of the merits of the colt was he that he did not even subject him to one of his trials before the Two Thousand. The Saturday previous to the race Dawson and Porter met on the Heath. Dawson, brimming over with enthusiasm for his charge, called up the lad on Minting saying to Porter as he did so that he was about to be shown the best horse he had ever seen in his life. Porter admired the big colt and then brought Ormonde along for inspection. Dawson would have none of it that Ormonde could possibly be the better. 'When they get to the Dip,' he said, 'it will be "Minting" and nothing else.' He had completely forgotten Archer's warning about Minting's dislike for a gradient.

Porter quietly pointed out the dangers of over-confidence and said that it might be just there, in the Dip, that Minting would be beaten.

In fact the only real worry Porter had about the race was concerning his jockey. For some reason undisclosed he was obliged to put up G. Barrett who, though a good enough horseman, was very much inclined to lose his head if he were pushed.

[173]

But in the event nothing mattered. Ormonde simply strode over his rivals leaving Minting toiling exactly where Porter had said he would—in the Dip. Saraband ran wretchedly with Archer to finish fourth just in front of the Duchess's St. Mirin.

Dawson's disappointment was so crushing especially after all his boasts which were so unusual for him to make that he went straight back to Exning, took to his bed and was not seen again in public for a week. But he accepted without hesitation that he had been wrong and that Minting would never beat Ormonde at equal weights. Immediately he took the colt out of the Derby. Archer's ability to divine the characteristics of the horses he rode and to know where they were likely to falter had been proved right once again. Dawson would have been a wiser and probably a richer man had he listened to Archer's warnings. He now decided to train Minting for the Grand Prix.

Peck was also disappointed in Saraband's showing and straight away took him, also, out of the Derby. This left Archer without a mount and Porter lost no time in securing him for Ormonde. Once more Porter, supremely confident, did not try Ormonde at home before the Derby.

Despite the result of the Two Thousand and the slamming by Ormonde of the good colts in the field General Williams retained his belief in The Bard. Williams, in fact, was every bit as confident with him as Dawson had been with Minting, nor did he learn from the other's defeat. He told his friends that with The Bard he had the beating of Ormonde and advised the whole of the Marlborough House set and the raffish cronies with whom he mixed, to back him. Peck, however, a wiser and more knowledgeable man, did not share this over-confidence. Nor did the public. Ormonde, started favourite at 9–4 on with The Bard second in the betting at 7–2 against.

The Bard, gallant little horse that he was, certainly made a fight of it. But Archer, as usual, had the inside at Tattenham Corner, gaining a couple of lengths by the way he came round it. The Bard tackled him in the straight when both horses were clear of their field. But Wood, on The Bard, was hard at his

[174]

mount while Archer had not moved on Ormonde. Once he did it was all over. Ormonde won without ever being really off the bit. St. Mirin was a bad third.

Like Dawson General Williams was bitterly disappointed. Unlike the trainer he sought to lay the blame for this defeat on his jockey. In fact no horse in training could have beaten Ormonde that day and the racing public recognized it by the storms of cheers with which they welcomed the favourite home.

After winning his fifth Derby Archer went over to Paris to ride Minting in the Grand Prix. At this time there was considerable hostility between the racing worlds of the two countries. That year feelings were running even higher than usual. Archer was warned that the French jockeys were determined to stop him and that if he did get through and win there might be trouble from the crowd. Bearing these warnings in mind he went, for once, the longest way round, lying last for a long time and then coming wide on the outside to make his run. The going was very heavy but even giving away so much ground Minting won easily, which alone emphasizes Ormonde's excellence. When the horses came back to the enclosure everyone connected with Minting took pains to get Archer through the scales and off the course in the least possible time but in fact the precautions were unnecessary for there was no trouble.

It was a great year for Porter since, in addition to having Ormonde in his stable, H.R.H. the Prince of Wales on the advice of Lord Alington decided to race on the flat and to send him his horses to train. The Prince commenced in a modest way with two fillies by Hermit, Counterpane and Lady Peggy. Porter started well for him. He entered Counterpane in a Maiden Plate at Sandown Park and gave Archer the honour of riding her. She came home an easy winner, so to his other laurels Archer could now add that of having ridden the Prince's first winner on the flat. To celebrate it and with the permission of H.R.H. he had himself photographed in the Royal colours. Later in the year, when he received the prints he presented one to the Prince and was sent a gracious acknowledgement from Abergeldie Castle where the Royal entourage was then in residence.

But, although winners were coming in, it was not being a great year for Archer. He was in ill-health, out of sorts, and the winners were not the right winners for his gambling was going desperately badly. At Manchester he dead-heated on Mignon with Wood on Monarch of the Glen and was beaten a head in the run-off. That year Sandown Park put on the first Eclipse Stakes worth £10,000 to the winner. It was the most valuable race of its kind to be put on in England up to that date. Minting was entered and was generally held to have it at his mercy although Bendigo was also in it, but Minting's leg filled just before the race and he had to be taken out, Archer rode Candlemas instead and was beaten three lengths by Cannon on Bendigo.

Ormonde won two races at Ascot and Porter then put him by for the St. Leger, making sure Archer would ride him. Despite the fact that by the time of the race he was afflicted in his wind, he started at 7–1 on and made hacks of his opponents, winning by four lengths without ever being asked to do more than canter. The remainder of Ormonde's career in so far as it affects Archer may be briefly summarized. Archer rode him in his next three-year-old races and won them all. At odds of 25–1 on he won the Great Foal Stakes at Newmarket. In the same week he walked over for the Newmarket St. Leger with Porter giving him a lead on his hack and some wag in the crowd shouting at him: 'Go on, John, he'll beat you!' He then won the Champion Stakes with odds of no less than 100–1 on him; he beat Mephisto and Theodore in the Free Handicap giving each of them 2 st. and wound up the season by walking over for the Private Sweepstakes, the owners of colts of such stature as Melton and The Bard paying a substantial forfeit rather than take him on. Ormonde then passes out of this story. Whether he was a greater racehorse than St. Simon must always be a matter for debate. Porter thought he was but then Porter, understandably, may well have been prejudiced. Certainly he did more than St. Simon was ever asked to do and probably beat better horses.

Unquestionably, however, St. Simon was by far the most successful at stud.

But all this is to anticipate. As Archer said, almost anyone could have won on Ormonde. For himself he believed, that season, that he was riding below his best form, that he was being beaten where he should not have been beaten and where a year or so back he would not have been. He was still in front of his nearest rival in the jockeys' list but nothing like so far in front as usual. In fact, earlier in the season, Wood had been ahead of him, the first and only occasion this had happened to him since 1873. Despondently, he told Watson he thought he was too far behind to catch up. It seemed unlikely that he would top the 200 mark this year and, if he did not, it would be the first time for ten years save for 1880 when he had only missed it by three and 1881 when he had been savaged by Muley Edris.

Needless to say he blamed himself for this run of bad luck and he worried and fretted about it. He could not stop betting, either, and he now thought it was interfering with his judgement. He was beaten on the favourite, Enterprise, in the Middle Park Plate. Enterprise was a useful two-year-old owned by Mr. Douglas Baird on whom Archer earlier in the year had won the July Stakes at Newmarket. Lord Calthorpe's Florentine beat him pretty easily in the Middle Park by two lengths. Analysing what had happened Archer decided that he had been wrong in making the running and thought he had ridden an ill-judged race. This self-criticism is evidence of the state of his mind at the time for it was almost certainly misconceived. It was not echoed by either the public or the Press, but his mental condition, aggravated by his physical weakness from wasting, made him think that he was the object of derision as a falling idol.

After the Middle Park he had to decide what to ride in the Cambridgeshire. It was, along with the Ascot Gold Cup, the only race of any consequence in the Calendar which he had never won. As a boy he had been beaten on the Truth Gelding and made a big gamble go wrong, last year he had been second. Now he was desperately anxious to win it for the first time to add it to his record and to rehabilitate himself in his own eyes for the mistakes he thought he had been making.

The Duchess's St. Mirin had been having an unlucky season. He was a good colt who might have been marked out for excellence in a lesser year. He was in the Cambridgeshire with 8 st. 6 lb. The Duchess thought she had every chance of winning and she wanted Archer to ride. Alec Taylor at Manton had another three-year-old in the stable called Carlton. This colt was leased to Lord Edward Somerset, the Duke of Beaufort's brother, and was also in the Cambridgeshire and fancied by his owner and his friends. Before the race Taylor tried the two colts and Carlton won the trial easily. Archer did not ride in the trial but he heard about it, made inquiries as to who had ridden St. Mirin and, finding it was an inexperienced boy, drew his own conclusions. The Duchess's blandishments, too, may have had something to do with it; at all events he decided to ride St. Mirin.

Shortly after making this decision Archer met A. E. T. Watson, the Editor of the *Sporting and Dramatic News*. During the conversation Archer told Watson that he would ride St. Mirin, that he did not accept the result of the trial as accurate and that he thought he would win. Dining that night at the Beefsteak Watson discussed the race with Beaufort with whom he was on very friendly terms. Beaufort and Watson had collaborated in the preparation of the Badminton Library, a collection of books on sport; Watson had stayed at Badminton on numerous occasions and hunted with Beaufort's hounds. He told the Duke what Archer had said.

Beaufort had the greatest admiration for Archer and, indeed, liking for him, but it is an indication of how some of those in high places were beginning to doubt his judgement that he dismissed the jockey's views without a second thought, telling Watson that they were 'absurdly wrong', that he had watched the trial himself and believed that the form there shown would work out on the racecourse.

Whatever anyone else said, and the result of the trial was by now common knowledge, Archer had convinced himself he was right and, as usual, was prepared to back his opinion with his money. He had decided that with St. Mirin his luck would turn. The colt was at a long price and he backed it heavily. Moreover he told his friends to do the same and made no secret of his belief in his chances. Then he went over to Ireland to ride Cambusmore at the Curragh October Meeting for the Lord Lieutenant, Lord Londonderry, to whom the colt had now been sold.

Before setting out, since there had been another spate of burglaries at Newmarket he told his valet to take out the revolver, see that it was in order and to sleep with it by his bed while Archer was away. Whenever Archer was back in residence the revolver was to be returned to the drawer in the pedestal table beside his bed.

Custance travelled with him to Ireland for he had been asked to act as starter to the meeting. There was quite a party of them and they stayed at the Shelbourne Hotel in St. Stephen's Green. Even then Custance was shocked by Archer's appearance.

Archer had no engagements on the first day but, since he had never ridden at the Curragh before, he went along with Custance to have a look at the course. He was recognized and given a tremendous reception. But he was worried about his weight and had Custance weigh him on the scales before racing. He was 9 st. 4 lb. without his jacket and waistcoat. He thought that this meant he had only to take off another pound to ride Cambusmore and then found that he had misread the conditions and that Cambusmore was in with only 9 st.

That evening, at the express invitation of the proprietor, they went to the theatre where the royal box was reserved for them and they saw *The Mikado*. A crowd was waiting for him when he left and they followed him back to the hotel shouting and cheering for 'the great Mr. Archer'.

In addition to riding Cambusmore for Lord Londonderry he had received a request to ride a good two-year-old of Mr. C. J. Blake's called Isidore at 8 st. 7 lb. Since everyone assured him it was a ready-made winner he was determined to do it.

[179]

Having no rides the following day, he spent it in the Turkish bath dosing himself with 'the mixture', though somehow he found time to have himself photographed, the last photograph, as it transpired, that was ever taken of him. On Thursday when he went down to the Curragh he still could not do 8 st. 7 lb. He was only able to weigh out at 8 st. 12 lb. Even so this meant he had taken off 6 lb. in twenty-four hours.

When he got up on Cambusmore and came out on to the course he was greeted with storms of cheering from every enclosure. Since it was his first ride in Ireland he badly wanted to make it a winning one. As usual he was down early at the post. Custance, watching him, thought he looked even worse than he had when they had met on the boat. 'Well, Fred,' he said to him. 'I don't know if it's the excitement from the ovation they gave you or the wasting you have done, but I never saw you look half so bad as you do now.'

Archer laughed and answered him: 'If I look bad now, how shall I look next Wednesday when I ride St. Mirin at 8 st. 6 lb. in the Cambridgeshire?'

Cambusmore duly won and so did Isidore but in the last race, a welter flat race, riding again for Mr. C. J. Blake he was beaten into third place by Tom Beasley and a Mr. Cullen. So Beasley joined 'Mr. Abingdon' as one of the few amateurs ever to have beaten the champion. The ovation that greeted Beasley for this feat nearly equalled that given Archer on his appearance.

Although Archer had quite made up his mind to ride St. Mirin he was in Ireland and away from the Duchess's immediate surveillance. She was determined to keep the pressure on him lest he alter his decision. She must have known very well that his friends were anxious about him and feared for his health as a result of his drastic wasting, but she wanted him on her horse in that race and what she wanted she usually got. Aware that while he was away efforts might be made to have him change his mind she sent him a telegram which was handed in that evening at the Shelbourne Hotel. It ran: *My horse runs in the Cambridgeshire. I count on you to ride it—Montrose.*

[180]

She was right to have her doubts and fears, for Custance, at least, was doing his best to dissuade him from riding at that weight. 'You don't mean to say you are going to ride 8 st. 6 lb. next week,' he said to him on the mail boat as they crossed back to England.

'Cus, I am sure to ride St. Mirin 8 st. 6 lb. or at most 8 st. 7 lb. I shall win the Cambridgeshire and then be able to come down into your country and enjoy myself this winter,' was Archer's reply.

Custance knew all about the effects of wasting and he again implored Archer not to keep on trying to do these ridiculous weights. If one could do it by exercise, he said, it was not so bad but he had seen so many jockeys wasting on physic 'go out like the snuff of a candle'.

'Never mind if I go out or not, I shall do it,' was all the answer he received.

On landing Custance promised to call to see him at Falmouth House when he came down for the Houghton Meeting. This he did, to be told by Mrs. Coleman, who was now keeping house for him, that Archer was in his Turkish bath. It was the morning of Tuesday, 26th October, the day of the Cambridgeshire.

Archer had, in fact, spent most of the intervening period, when not on the racecourse, in the Turkish bath and his diet had consisted almost entirely of huge doses of 'the mixture'. Indeed for three days before the Cambridgeshire he touched no food of any sort and, although he had ridden a winner for the Duchess the day before, he was now admitting to feeling weak and ill, which was most unlike him.

'I have never ridden the winner of the Cambridgeshire,' he told a friend. 'And if I don't succeed this time I shall never try again.'

Custance did not meet him until they greeted each other in the weighing-room. He said he thought he had never seen him look so badly and it is to be remembered that he had been with him and commented on his appearance three weeks before. But Archer seemed outwardly, at all events, to be cheerful enough and they laughed together over some of the events of their trip to Ireland.

Watson met him, too, in the Birdcage, just before the race, and asked him about it. Archer told him that St. Mirin would win and that if he had backed Carlton he was wrong. Watson went off to the Duke of Beaufort's carriage and repeated this conversation. The Duke said once more that he did not know what had happened to Archer's judgement, that he knew Archer had gambled heavily on St. Mirin, that the trial was right, Carlton would win and Archer would lose his money.

Lambton, wondering about all these stories and knowing Archer as a friend, asked him his opinion about the two horses. With typical good sense Archer pointed out that there had been an inexperienced boy on St. Mirin in the trial, that there was one now, Woodburn, on Carlton and that Carlton was a difficult horse to ride in a race. He reckoned these factors, combined with his own skill, should turn the tables in St. Mirin's favour. He overlooked, however, that, despite his endeavours, he was still a pound overweight and that he was far weaker than he should have been.

Melton with Tom Cannon on his back was also in the race. Archer discounted Melton entirely for these days he had taken a dislike to racing and only on rare occasions would he show his true form. Going down to the post Cannon, who had not ridden Melton before, asked Archer about him. 'You are on just about the biggest thief in England, Tom,' Archer told him and went on to describe what Melton did when he was not trying. This perhaps, may not have been very wise of him. He was certainly in a most peculiar state of mind, strung-up, over-confident, and, for once, too talkative.

Carlton started favourite at 425–100. St. Mirin, because of the stories and rumours, despite Archer's known belief in him, was at the long price of 100–8.

The race was run at a great pace for those days. At the distance Carlton was leading, with St. Mirin and Melton behind him. When both of them came and collared Carlton, Woodburn went for his whip. Carlton then cracked and was done with. But Cannon seemed to have persuaded Melton to race. At all events he was going far too well for Archer's peace of mind. He began to get at St. Mirin. Melton, seriously asked to run on, threw up his head and dropped back, out of it. St. Mirin then appeared to have the race at his mercy.

On Beaufort's carriage the Duke and Watson were gloomily telling each other that Archer had been right after all when suddenly, on the far side of the course, something came at St. Mirin and caught him. Challenged, Archer drove St. Mirin on as only he knew how. They passed the post so close together no one could say who had won. All anyone knew was that the other horse was an unconsidered outsider Sailor Prince, a six-year-old who was getting a stone from St. Mirin.

As he stepped off the scale and in the heat of the moment Archer said he thought he had won but an instant later he changed his mind. While they waited for the result he told Sir George Chetwynd that he had been beaten. He was right. Sailor Prince had won by a head. He had lost his tremendous bet, lost the Duchess her stake and failed to win the Cambridgeshire for the first time. In a way it was almost an exact repetition of that race twelve years before when as a boy he had wasted too hard and been beaten a neck on the Truth Gelding.

Of course he blamed himself. He had allowed Cannon to 'kid' him, he said, and had taken on Melton too soon thus giving Sailor Prince an opportunity of sitting behind and pouncing on him. He did not appear to realize that it was almost certainly his privations which cost him and the Duchess the race. He was a weak, sick man and had he been himself the tremendous strength and drive which had brought him home successfully in so many desperate finishes would in all probability have carried the day.

He preferred to blame his judgement. He had ridden it wrong, he said. More than ever, now, he was depressed and cast down.

Worse still, rumour got to work again. For some extraordinary reason the Somersets, who were friends and admirers of

Archer's, convinced themselves that he had something to do with their horse losing the race. Lord Edward Somerset told Lambton that he 'knew' Archer had given Woodburn a large sum of money to throw the race away. On being challenged by Lambton, who would have no word spoken against a friend, to produce evidence of this, he backed down, admitting that he only had it from rumour and hearsay. But that encounter did not stop him and his brother from talking. Later that winter Watson met Beaufort at the theatre and Beaufort gave Watson what was, so he said, the 'true history' of the race. But Beaufort and his brother had lost large sums themselves on the result and, in racing, disappointment coupled with financial loss frequently conspire together to distort judgement and obscure truth.

Needless to say, Archer knew that his old friends and admirers—had not Beaufort three years before written personally to him, imploring him to ride his horse Eastern Emperor—*will you write me a line to Manton House, Marlborough, and say you can ride him? I have tried for thirty years and more to win the Criterion . . .* —had turned against him. And then, on the Friday of that same week, came the final blow of the break with Machell.

Whether Machell heard the rumours and was influenced by them no one can tell. At all events Archer told him to back a horse, Queen Bee, in the Seller on Friday. Archer rode five winners out of nine races that Friday but on Queen Bee he was beaten a head by Wood on General Williams's Draycot. A lady friend of Machell's said on the stand that Archer had told her not to back his mount. As for almost everyone else in racing that Newmarket week had been a bad one for Machell. He was badly hit and knew that Archer was, too. As is the way with moody and sensitive people when things go wrong Machell forgot all Archer had done for him in the past and, brooding on this information, convinced himself he had been tricked. He met Archer in the paddock and turned his back on him. One of the longest associations and firmest friendships in racing was broken by the casual word of a silly woman setting a suspicious nature alight. After what had gone before in the way of slights, rebuffs and rumours this was almost more than Archer could bear.

His final winner on Friday was in the last race and it was the last winner he ever rode. By a coincidence it was on a horse called Blanchard belonging to Lord Falmouth, one of the few he still kept in training. It was fitting indeed that his last winning ride should be in the magpie jacket he had worn to so many splendid triumphs.

But it was, at the time, precious little consolation. The public insult by Machell cut him more deeply than anything else, especially since he knew it to be unjust. Afterwards, when it was too late, Machell admitted that for him to have persuaded himself that Archer was not trying when he was only beaten by the shortest of short heads was a piece of ludicrous stupidity, as indeed it was. Quite incidentally, it is also an example of the state of mind which a run of failures and disappointments can induce in even the most experienced of racing men.

At the end of the meeting Archer went back to Falmouth House wretched and depressed. He was in low spirits and complained of not feeling well. The malaise continued and may indeed have been the beginning of his final, fatal illness. He refused a dinner invitation from Lord Cairns, *only a few people and no reporters*, and he did not go to Lincoln at the beginning of the following week. For him to miss a meeting was almost unheard of, and this alone demonstrates his physical and mental condition.

But he had promised to ride at Brighton on Wednesday. Ill though he was, he determined to fulfil the engagement. His personal score now stood at 170 and with a run of luck he thought he might better the 200 once again. But he could not win a race during the two days of the Brighton Meeting. In fact on the second day he was beaten on two short-priced favourites, The Warden at 11–4 against and Mohawk 9–4 against. It was early November and bitterly cold on the exposed Brighton Downs. He complained of a feverish chill, but he had promised to ride another fancied horse at Lewes the next day. Instead of seeing a doctor who he was sure would order him back to bed, he went on to Lewes.

At Lewes Lambton met him and talked to him and thought he looked dreadfully ill. He went out on an odds-on favourite, Tommy Tittlemouse, the last horse he was ever to ride on a racecourse, and was beaten out of a place. When he came in the fever had him in such a hold that even his determined spirit and desire to ride winners was compelled to give it best. He told his friends that he would ride no more that day but was going straight back to Falmouth House and, once there, to bed. More surprising still in one such as he, when Gurry, the trainer, came up to speak to him, he asked him to travel back to Newmarket in his company saying that he felt so ill he feared he might collapse.

Gurry looked at him and promptly agreed. When they got to Liverpool Street Archer had a basin of arrowroot with brandy in it. During the journey to Cambridge he fell asleep and, when he awoke, declared that he felt much better. Gurry accompanied him to Falmouth House where his sister, Mrs. Coleman, and Captain Bowling were waiting for him. They insisted on his going straight to bed which he did.

Hearing that his master was returning the valet had taken the revolver from his own room and put it into the drawer of Archer's bedside pedestal as he had been instructed.

The following morning it was obvious that whatever improvement he had mentioned to Gurry on the train the night before had been only temporary. He was, in fact, very much worse. Dr. Wright of Newmarket who had been attending him on and off for fourteen years and who had originally made up 'the mixture' was sent for. On arrival he found Archer's temperature very high indeed; he was restless and in a bad fever. Wright stayed with him most of the morning. Archer was not delirious and he was lucid enough for the doctor to suggest taking a second opinion. Archer refused to consent to this but later on Wright decided that it was essential and accepted the responsibility of calling in Dr. Latham of Cambridge. Early the following morning they visited the patient together. His temperature had not come down and at times his mind was now rambling. He was under some sort of delusion about food and would take no medicine saying that he only wanted 'the mixture'.

The doctors issued a joint bulletin stating their charge was suffering from the effects of a severe chill following a high fever. The next day the fever appeared to be subsiding but during the night he worsened again. When they consulted on Monday the doctors diagnosed typhoid. The following bulletin was then issued: *Newmarket. November 8th. 1886. Mr. Fred Archer is suffering from an attack of typhoid fever. There is an improvement in his symptoms today—signed, J. R. Wright.*

Two nurses were engaged to help Mrs. Coleman look after him. Indeed she and Captain Bowling had their hands full enough dealing with callers, letters and telegrams. Falmouth, ever kindly and thoughtful, sent a reply prepaid wire to Mrs. Coleman calling her brother by his Christian name alone; Hastings, too, was amongst the many others who sent telegrams of urgent inquiry.

The improvement in his condition was maintained but, although physically he was getting better, he was in a state of deep mental depression. He kept telling the doctors and nurses that he was going to die. When Charlotte Harrington, one of the nurses, tried to reassure him, 'I wish I was your way of thinking,' he said to her. She then thought him rational enough and quite coherent but suffering terrible depression of spirits.

Dr. Wright had a long talk with him that Monday morning. By this time his temperature had come down and his condition was very much better. The doctor found him quite clear in his mind but still possessed by the idea that he was going to die. Wright did his best to lift him out of his low spirits and told him of his marked and rapid physical improvement. He left the house about 9.30 to continue his calls.

During the morning the nurses stayed with him and Mrs. Coleman and Captain Bowling were continually in and out of the sick-room. At twelve o'clock Captain Bowling left the house on some errand. Mrs. Coleman remained in the room. Shortly after two she told Donnington, the other nurse, to go downstairs for her dinner. Charlotte Harrington remained in the room. She opened a bottle of eau-de-Cologne and put it beside the bed. Then Archer asked Mrs. Coleman to send the nurse away as he had something private to say to her. This had happened before during the illness and Mrs. Coleman did not see anything unusual in the request. She asked Harrington to go downstairs for a few minutes. She then looked out of the window and waited for her brother to speak.

'Are they coming?' he said to her.

Turning round she saw that he was half out of bed and that he had a revolver in his hand. It was in his left hand. She rushed towards him and tried to obtain possession of it.

They grappled together. 'He seemed awfully strong,' she said. Putting his right arm round her neck to support himself he raised the revolver with his left hand to his head. The struggle had forced her back against the door, closing it, so that her screams went unheard. Then he pulled the trigger. He was dead before help could reach him.

The genius which had flashed so briefly and so brilliantly across the racecourses of England was extinguished. The wonderful career was over; the bright day was done.

He was only twenty-nine years of age. He had known triumph, heartbreak, tragedy, high achievement, public adulation, and had let none of these overcome him. In the end it was physical weakness brought on by wasting, and his own temperament which beat him. Of him it can be said with truth that no one could have conquered him but himself.

Over a quarter of a century afterwards Lambton, the aristocrat, recalling his association with Archer, the uneducated stableboy from Prestbury who had made himself into a world figure, said of him: 'He was certainly the most attractive figure that I have ever come across on a racecourse and, apart from my admiration of him as a jockey, I was very fond of him as a man. . . . Archer had, of course, his enemies and detractors, and rumour and scandal did not spare him; but I believe the best answer to these charges is the fact that, once a stable, owner or trainer employed him, they continued to do so as long as he lived, and to the end he retained the confidence of the public. The men he rode for and associated with, whether in a high or low station of life, were always the straight people of the Turf. He, like Mat Dawson, had no use for the bad men, and he avoided them.'

Let that be his epitaph.

Appendix

Here is the record and it is worth looking at: Born 11th January 1857. Died 8th November 1886. Champion Jockey 1874–1886.

TABLE OF MOUNTS AND VICTORIES

Year	Mounts	Wins	Year	Mounts	Wins
1870	15	2	1879	568	197
1871	40	3	1880	362	120
1872	180	27	1881	532	220
1873	422	107	1882	560	210
1874	530	147	1883	631	232
1875	605	172	1884	577	241
1876	662	207	1885	667	246
1877	602	218	1886	512	170
1878	619	229			

Total mounts: 8,004. Total wins: 2,748.

Classic wins: Derby 5, St. Leger 6, Oaks 4, 2,000 Guineas 4, 1,000 Guineas 2. TOTAL 21.

Other principal races won: Grand Prix de Paris 3, French Derby 2, City and Suburban 5, Great Metropolitan 1, Cesarewitch 2, Woodcote Stakes 6, Clearwell Stakes 8, Middle Park

Plate 3, Dewhurst Plate 5, Great Ebor Handicap 2, Champagne Stakes 7, Portland Plate 2, Liverpool Autumn Cup 3, Royal Hunt Cup 3, Prince of Wales Stakes Ascot 3, Alexandra Plate 2.

His will was proved at £60,000.

Bibliography

❧

WILLIAM ALLISON, *My Kingdom for a Horse*. G. Richards. 1919.

WILLIAM ALLISON, *Memories of Men and Horses*. G. Richards. 1922.

SIR J. D. ASTLEY, Bt., *Fifty Years of My Life* (2 vols.). Hurst and Blackett Ltd. 1894.

ARTHUR M. BINSTEAD and ERNEST WELLS, *A Pink'un and A Pelican*. Everett. 1898.

ARTHUR M. BINSTEAD. *Pitcher in Paradise*. Sands. 1903.

T. H. BIRD, *Admiral Rous and the English Turf 1795–1877*. Putnam & Co. Ltd. 1939

J. B. BOOTH, *Old Pink'un Days*. G. Richards. 1924.

J. B. BOOTH, *'Master' and Men. Pink'un Yesterdays*. T. Werner Laurie Ltd. 1927.

J. B. BOOTH, *Pink Parade, the Pink'un World*. Butterworth & Co. Ltd. 1933.

J. B. BOOTH, *Sporting Times*. T. Werner Laurie Ltd. 1938.

J. B. BOOTH, *Life Laughter and Brass Hats*. T. Werner Laurie Ltd. 1939.

MAI BOVILL and GEORGE R. ASKWITH, *Roddy Owen: A Memoir*. John Murray Ltd. 1897.

ALGERNON CECIL, *Queen Victoria and Her Prime Ministers*. Eyre and Spottiswoode. 1952.

PATRICK R. CHALMERS, *Racing England*. B. T. Batsford Ltd. 1939.

N   [193]

'A Cheltonian', *Autobiographies of the Three Archers*. S. H. Brookes, Cheltenham. 1885.

Sir G. Chetwynd, Bt. *Racing Reminiscences and Experiences of the Turf* (2 vols.). Longmans, Green & Co. Ltd. 1891.

Sir Theodore Cook, *History of the English Turf*. H. Virtue & Co. 1901–1904.

Harding Cox, *Chasing and Racing*. John Lane. 1922.

B. W. R. Curling, *British Racecourses*. H. F. & G. Witherby Ltd. 1951.

Henry Custance, *Riding Recollections and Turf Stories*. Edward Arnold Ltd. 1894.

Sam Darling, *Reminiscences*. Mills and Boon Ltd. 1914.

Sydenham Dixon, *From Gladiateur to Persimmon*. G. Richards. 1901.

J. S. Fletcher, *The History of the St. Leger Stakes*. Hutchinson & Co. 1902.

Meyrick Good, *The Lure of the Turf*. Odhams Press Ltd. 1957.

Meyrick Good, *Good Days*. Hutchinson & Co. 1941.

John Hislop, *The Turf*. Wm. Collins, Sons & Co. Ltd. 1957.

George Hodgman. *Sixty Years on the Turf*. Grant Richards. 1901.

E. M. Humphris, *The Life of Fred Archer*. Hutchinson & Co. 1923.

E. M. Humphris, *The Life of Mathew Dawson*. H. F. & G. Witherby. 1928.

R. Rhodes-James, *Rosebery*. Weidenfeld and Nicolson Ltd. 1963.

B. de Sales La Terrière, *Days that are Gone*. Hutchinson & Co. 1924.

George Lambton, *Men and Horses I Have Known*. Butterworth & Co. Ltd. 1924. Later edition: J. A. Allen & Co. Ltd.

Anita Leslie, *The Fabulous Leonard Jerome*. Hutchinson & Co. 1954.

R. C. Lyle, *Royal Newmarket*. Putnam & Co. Ltd. 1945.

Alan Macey, *The Romance of the Derby Stakes*. Hutchinson & Co. 1930.

Richard Marsh, *A Trainer to Two Kings*. Cassell & Co. Ltd. 1925.

Edward Moorhouse, *The Romance of the Derby* (2 vols.). Biographical Press. 1908.

Charles Morton, *My Sixty Years on the Turf*. Hutchinson & Co. Undated.

Roger Mortimer, *The Jockey Club*. Cassell & Co. Ltd. 1958.

Roger Mortimer, *The History of the Derby Stakes*. Cassell & Co. Ltd. 1962.

John Porter, *Kingsclere*. Chatto & Windus Ltd. 1896.

John Porter (with Edward Moorhouse), *John Porter of Kingsclere*. G. Richards. 1919.

Duke of Portland, *Memories of Racing and Hunting.* Faber & Faber Ltd. 1935.

Duke of Portland, *Men, Women and Things*. Faber & Faber Ltd. 1937.

Gordon Richards, *My Story*. Hodder & Stoughton Ltd. 1955.

John Maunsell Richardson, *Gentlemen Riders Past and Present*. Vinton. 1909.

M. E. Richardson, *The Life of a Great Sportsman*. Vinton. 1919.

Lord Rossmore, *Things I Can Tell*. Eveleigh Nash. 1912.

Frank Siltzer, *Newmarket*. Cassell & Co. Ltd. 1923.

Fred Smith, *The Glorious Uncertainty of Horse Racing*. Privately printed (undated).

Earl of Suffolk (Editor), *The Badminton Library—Racing*. Longmans, Green & Co. Ltd. 1886.

Thormanby, *Kings of the Turf*. Hutchinson & Co. 1898.

A. E. T. Watson, *The Turf*. Lawrence and Bullen. 1898.

A. E. T. Watson, *A Sporting and Dramatic Career*. Macmillan & Co. Ltd. 1918.

CHARLES ADOLPH VOIGT, *Famous Gentlemen Riders at Home and Abroad*. Hutchinson & Co. 1925.
The Racing Calendar.

NEWSPAPERS AND PERIODICALS

The Times.
The *Morning Post.*
The *Illustrated Sporting and Dramatic News.*
The *Sporting Times.*
The *World.*
The *Winning Post.*
The *Strand Magazine.*
Bailey's Magazine.
Bell's Life in London.
The *British Racehorse.*

Index

Archer, Frederick James—*cont.*
as 'the tinman', 39; as gambler, 40, 41; successes in eighteenth year, 40; great series of wins, 40–1; relations with Capt. Machell, 43–5, 47, 85, 114, 115, 184; great 1876 record, 47; increasing public admiration for, 48; successes of 1877–8, 49, 53–7; the Archer-Falmouth-Dawson triumvirate, 49 seqq.; and Sir George Chetwynd, 49; wins Derby on Silvio, 52; wins 1877 St. Leger, 52; his record by end of 1878, 57; mental conflicts of, 58–9; early 1879 successes of, in Classics, 63; Duke of Beaufort's assessment of, 64; Chetwynd's assessment of, 69, 70; Duke of Portland describes as rider to hounds, 70; and Lord Wilton, 70; and Dukes of Portland and Westminster, 72–7; and Lord Rosebery, 74–6; and Duke of Beaufort, 64, 75; and Lord Hastings, 76; savaged by Muley Edris, 77–9; the 1880 Derby and French Prix du Jockey Club, 84; lost time through injury in 1880, 84–5; and Baird, 86–7; record for 1880, 87; great year of 1881, 88–106; becomes engaged to Helen Dawson, 107; starts the Newmarket Drag, 107; on the excellence of Wheel of Fortune, 65; becomes Dawson's partner, 88; financial status of, 107–8; women attracted to, 89 (*and see* Montrose, Duchess of); builds Falmouth House, 108, 114, 120; first scandal (1882), 108; dislike for racing in France, 112–13; close friends of, 114–15; first coolness with Mat Dawson, 112; and the 1882 St. Leger, 116–19; his 1882 record of successes, 120–5, 136; marriage of, 120–1; analysis of the 1882 Derby scandal, 127–30; in France in 1882, 130, 131; increasing worries, 136–7; birth and death of son, 138; breach with Portland, 139; worries in 1884 season, 140; accused, with Wood, of operating jockeys' ring, 142; recovers his luck, 144–7; troubles of 1884 Cambridgeshire week, 147–50; birth of daughter, 151; death of wife, 151; visits America with Bartholomew and Bowling, 152–4; will of, 153–5, 192; returns to racing, 156; establishes record to stand until 1933, 168; his 1886 season, 172–85; and Dawson's retirement, 171–2; wins his fifth Derby, 174–5; in France, 1886, 175; rides Prince of Wales's first winner on flat, 175; and St. Mirin, 180–4; breaks with Machell, 184; last winning ride, 185; last illness and suicide, 185–9; record of principal victories of his career, 191

Archer, William (Fred Archer's father), 11; in Russia, as manager of Emperor's stud, 11–12; marries Emma Hayward, 12; career of in England, 11–12; at the 'King's Arms', 12, 13; trains Fred in early years, 13–16; takes Fred to Mat Dawson, 15–16; birth of sons of, 12; becomes insatiable for money, 39; as landlord of Andoversford hotel, 47; further demands on Fred, 107, 136

Archer, William, first-born of above, 12; death of, 56

Archiduc, 148

Ascot, 36, 38, *and see* named events, e.g. Gold Cup

[207]